Love and Dishes

Love and Dishes

∾

Scene-Stealing Recipes
from Your Favorite Soap Stars

Edited by Irene Krause Keene

Hearst Books
New York

Library of Congress Cataloging-in-Publication Data

Love and dishes : scene-stealing recipes from your favorite soap stars / [edited] by Irene Krause Keene.
    p. cm.
  ISBN 0-688-12899-8
  1. Cookery.   2. Television actors and actresses — United States — Miscellanea.
3. Soap operas — United States — Miscellanea.
I. Keene, Irene Krause.
TX714.L677   1996
641.5 — dc20   95-33182
                                            CIP

Printed in the United States of America

First Edition

1   2   3   4   5   6   7   8   9   10

BOOK DESIGN BY LEAH CARLSON

Contents

❦

INTRODUCTION vii

The Opening Act
Appetizers, Soups, and Salads 1

Romantic Meals
*Chicken, Fish, Pasta, and Vegetarian
Main Dishes* 15

A Gathering of Suspects
Comfort Foods for Any Occasion 57

Cliffhangers
Desserts 77

Contributors' Profiles 95

INDEX 123

Introduction

∼

The most compelling stories on soap operas have a strong beginning, a convoluted middle, and, we hope, no end. The same is true for a really fine meal, whether it's breakfast for two or a Thanksgiving feast for forty.

Our favorite soap stars have real lives, too—and they're just like us. They eat, they sleep, they car-pool their kids, and they pay taxes. And they cook. We've asked a select group of actors to send in their favorite recipes for you. We hope you enjoy them.

Love and Dishes

the
Opening
Act

❦

Appetizers, Soups, and Salads

Appetizers set the stage for the rest of the meal. The lighter ones pique our interest, enticing us for what's to follow, while the more substantial starters are so satisfying that they are almost meals in themselves. Some of the recipes in this chapter, such as Monika's Minestrone and Pink Delight, do double duty—they are perfect for lunch before your favorite show begins.

Alexia Robinson, formerly Meg Lawson of
GENERAL HOSPITAL

Alexia's Stuffed Mushrooms

MAKES 4 SERVINGS

༄

20 fresh medium mushrooms

4 tablespoons butter

$^1/_2$ large onion, chopped

2 celery stalks, finely chopped

4 garlic cloves

$^1/_2$ cup chopped scallions

4 ounces crabmeat
(imitation or snowcrab),
flaked

4 ounces baby shrimp, minced

4 ounces baby scallops, minced

$^1/_4$ cup dry white wine

Fresh tarragon to taste

1 teaspoon dried tarragon

Salt and pepper

$^1/_2$ cup plain bread crumbs

Juice of 1 lemon (optional)

1. Preheat the oven to 350°F.

2. Wipe the mushrooms clean and discard stems.

3. Heat the butter in a large skillet and sauté onion, celery, and garlic until the onion is translucent, about 5 minutes.

4. Add scallions, crabmeat, shrimp, and scallops and cook for 3 minutes. Stir in the wine, tarragon, and salt and pepper to taste.

5. Stuff the mixture into the mushroom caps and top with bread crumbs.

6. Place the mushrooms in a buttered 13 x 9-inch baking dish. Squeeze lemon juice on top of the mushrooms if desired. Bake for 20 minutes or until the tops are lightly browned. Serve hot.

ᕫᕬ

Melody Thomas Scott, Nikki Abbott of
THE YOUNG AND THE RESTLESS

Melody Thomas Scott's Layered Southern Salad

MAKES 4 TO 6 SERVINGS

❧

1 head lettuce of choice, finely shredded

4 to 6 scallions, chopped

2 cans (5 ounces) water chestnuts, chopped

4 or 5 celery stalks, chopped

1 package (10 ounces) frozen peas

1 cup mayonnaise, preferably cold-pressed (available at most health food stores) or Miracle Whip

1 tablespoon sugar

8 slices bacon, cooked and crumbled

3 hard-boiled eggs, sliced

1 cup shredded cheddar cheese

1. Layer the lettuce, scallions, water chestnuts, celery, and peas in a large pan or casserole dish.

2. Spread mayonnaise on top of the peas to seal in the vegetables.

3. Sprinkle sugar on top and cover with plastic wrap. Refrigerate overnight.

4. When ready to serve, garnish the mixture with bacon bits, egg slices, and cheese shreds. Spoon onto individual plates and toss each serving separately.

"Everyone loves it, especially me."

Vanessa Marcil, Brenda Barrett of
GENERAL HOSPITAL

Vanessa's Salsa

MAKES 4 TO 8 SERVINGS

~

3 ripe tomatoes, diced

4 to 6 jalapeño peppers, diced

¹/₂ cup chopped fresh cilantro

1 large scallion, diced

¹/₂ cup olive oil

Juice of 1 lemon

Salt and pepper

Garlic powder

1. In a large bowl, combine the tomatoes, jalapeños, cilantro, and scallion. Add the olive oil and lemon juice. Season to taste with salt and pepper and garlic powder. Chill for 2 to 3 hours, then serve.

*"Great as a dip, with Mexican food or with
any meal. I enjoy making the salsa because of its fresh
ingredients and the fact that I am a vegetarian. This recipe
has been handed down from my great-grandfather
to my Grandmother Sally."*

Lisa Peluso, formerly Ava Masters of
LOVING

Escarole Soup

MAKES 6 TO 8 SERVINGS

1 chicken, about 3½ pounds
1½ large onions, finely chopped
1 bunch celery
7 large carrots
3 heads escarole, cleaned and chopped
1 pound ground meat (a mixture of equal portions of veal, pork, and beef)
2 eggs

Plain bread crumbs
½ to ¾ cup grated Parmesan cheese
Salt and pepper
1 box small soup pasta (for example, pastina, Anci-pepe, tiny bows, or rosamarina; do not use those meant for infants)

continued

The Opening Act

1. Fill a large stockpot three-quarters full with water.

2. Place the chicken in the pot and boil about 40 minutes, until a white foam forms on top. Skim off foam. Add 1 onion, celery, and carrots and let simmer. Meanwhile, in a separate large pot, bring water to a boil with a little salt. Add the escarole and boil for 10 minutes, until slightly wilted; don't overcook. Drain the escarole and add to the soup. Simmer for 1 hour.

3. While the soup is simmering, make small meatballs. In a large mixing bowl, combine and knead the ground meat, eggs, and remaining chopped 1/2 onion. Add enough bread crumbs to make the mixture firm enough to hold together. Add Parmesan cheese and salt and pepper to taste. Knead and roll into bite-size balls.

4. In a large skillet, brown the meatballs on all sides; drain excess oil and lay on paper towels to absorb additional grease. Remove the chicken from the soup and set aside to cool. Add the meatballs to the soup and simmer for 10 minutes.

5. When the chicken is cool, remove the meat from the bones and break into small pieces, discarding the skin and bones. Return the chicken to the soup, adding a little salt and pepper to taste.

6. In a large pot of salted boiling water, cook the pasta until tender, about 10 minutes. Drain and hold the pasta on the side until ready to serve. (Stir a ladle of soup broth into the pasta so it doesn't stick while waiting.)

7. Mash the carrots in the soup with a fork. Add the pasta to the soup and serve.

> "*This is a great holiday soup and just an incredible handy soup to make a big batch of and have around any time of the year. It is truly a meal in itself. You'll have to use your culinary expertise with this recipe because it was passed down from generation to generation in an Italian family (namely mine), and if you know anything about how Italian grandmothers cook, they never measure anything; magically, they seem to know how to throw in exactly enough of this or that to make it just right. I've had to learn by trial and error myself with this one, but I must say, when it turns out right, there's nothing that will delight your taste buds, or those of your guests, more than this soup. It has been a staple of every holiday meal in my family, ever since I was a little girl, and I can't imagine a holiday without it.*"

The Opening Act

Monika Schnarre, formerly Ivana of
THE BOLD AND THE BEAUTIFUL

Monika's Minestrone

MAKES 6 TO 8 SERVINGS

⁓

$1/3$ cup olive or vegetable oil

4 tablespoons butter
  or margarine

1 large onion, diced

2 large carrots, diced

2 celery stalks, diced

2 medium potatoes, diced

$1/2$ pound green beans,
  cut into 1-inch pieces

6 cups water

$1/2$ small head green cabbage,
  shredded

1 can (16 ounces) tomatoes

2 medium zucchini, diced

3 beef bouillon cubes

1 teaspoon salt

1 can (20 ounces) cannellini
  beans, drained

1 can (20 ounces) kidney
  beans, drained

$1/2$ cup grated Parmesan or
  Romano cheese

1. In a large pot or Dutch oven, heat the oil and butter over medium heat.

2. Add the onion, carrots, celery, potatoes, and green beans. Cook until lightly brown, about 20 minutes, stirring occasionally.

3. Add the water, cabbage, tomatoes with liquid, zucchini, bouillon cubes, and salt.

4. Bring to a boil, stirring to break up the tomatoes, then reduce heat to low, cover, and simmer 40 minutes or until all the vegetables are tender, stirring occasionally. Do not overcook.

5. Stir in the canned beans and cook 15 minutes longer or just until the soup is slightly thickened.

6. Ladle the soup into bowls and sprinkle with cheese.

"As a healthy alternative, cook the vegetables in water (eliminating oil and butter) and do not add the cheese in the final step. This gives you a low-fat tasty soup that I enjoy myself year-round."

Patricia Elliott, Renée Buchanan of
ONE LIFE TO LIVE

Pink Delight

MAKES 8 SERVINGS

10 small beets, peeled and
   thinly sliced

3 tablespoons finely cut chives

2 teaspoons dried dill

1 1/2 teaspoons salt

1/2 teaspoon pepper

1/4 cup apple juice

2 cups sour cream

1 cucumber, scored with a
   knife and thinly sliced

16 to 20 medium shrimp,
   peeled, cooked, and
   deveined

1. The day before serving, cook the beets in a medium pot over medium heat until tender, about 15 to 20 minutes. Reserve the cooking liquid.

2. In a large container, place the beets, cooking liquid, chives, dill, salt, pepper, apple juice, and 1/2 cup of the sour cream. Mix well, cover, and refrigerate for 1 to 2 hours.

3. When you are ready to serve, add enough cold water to the liquid to make 2 quarts and add the cucumbers.

4. Transfer the mixture to a large serving dish or soup tureen, and float dollops of $1/2$ cup sour cream on top.

5. Place the shrimp and the remaining 1 cup sour cream in separate serving bowls and let the guests help themselves.

> "*This is an incredibly rich cold soup for a hot summer or late evening meal. It is also wonderful for a candlelight supper for two. I call it Pink Delight, my version of the simpler borscht.*"

romantic
Meals

❦

Chicken, Fish, Pasta, and Vegetarian Main Dishes

These entrees are not just for lovers! The recipes are perfect for family meals, parties, and even to set the stage for seduction. No self-respecting soap would leave out passion and romance—and neither would we. But you're sure to find the right recipe whether the occasion is an intimate evening for two or a family supper.

Rebecca Holden, formerly Elena Parsons of
GENERAL HOSPITAL

King Ranch Chicken

MAKES 4 TO 6 SERVINGS

༄

1 chicken, about 3½ pounds

3 to 4 corn tortillas, cut
   into thirds

1 medium onion, chopped

4 stalks celery

4 tablespoons melted butter

2 cans (10½ ounces each)
   cream of chicken soup,
   undiluted

½ can (10-ounce size)
   Ro-Tel tomatoes and
   green chiles

1 cup shredded cheddar cheese

1. Preheat oven to 350°F.

2. Boil the chicken until cooked. Bone and cut the meat into
bite-size pieces. Let cool.

3. Line the bottom of a skillet with half the tortilla pieces, then top with the chicken pieces.

4. Sauté the onion and celery in butter until translucent, about 5 minutes. Sprinkle on top of the chicken.

5. Spread the soup on top, and add another layer of tortillas.

6. Spread the tomatoes and chiles on top and cover with the cheese.

7. Bake for 1 hour, or until the center bubbles.

Optional: $\frac{1}{2}$ cup sour cream may be added to the soup.

> "*This is an old Texas recipe with flavors that remind me of home. Guys always seem to love it. You can give them the leftovers to take home, and they'll think of you for days afterward.*"

Joseph Mascolo, Stefano Di Mera of
DAYS OF OUR LIVES

Chicken with Orange

MAKES 4 SERVINGS

❧

3- to 3¹/₂-pound fryer, cut up

2 tablespoons vegetable oil

2 medium onions, thinly sliced

4 medium carrots, cut into ¹/₂-inch slices

1 celery stalk, cut into 1-inch pieces

1 garlic clove

¹/₂ teaspoon dried marjoram

¹/₂ teaspoon dried oregano

1 can (10¹/₂ ounces) condensed chicken broth

³/₄ cup dry white wine

1 teaspoon Worcestershire sauce

1 tablespoon cornstarch

¹/₂ cup sour cream

³/₄ cup orange juice

¹/₂ teaspoon grated orange peel

Cooked rice

1. In a Dutch oven, cook the chicken in the oil, turning occasionally, until browned, about 6 minutes. Transfer the chicken to a plate.

2. Add the vegetables and garlic to the pot. Cook until brown, about 10 minutes. Add the herbs, broth, wine, and Worcestershire sauce.

3. Return the chicken to the Dutch oven and cover. Simmer over low heat until cooked through, about 30 minutes.

4. Transfer the chicken to a plate and keep warm.

5. Strain the liquid through a sieve and place vegetables aside. Over high heat, reduce the cooking liquid to 1 cup.

6. Return the vegetables to the Dutch oven and stir to coat with sauce.

7. In a small bowl, combine the cornstarch and sour cream. Stir into the vegetables. Add the orange juice and peel.

8. Cover the Dutch oven and cook until thickened, about 10 minutes. Stir once before serving. Serve the vegetables and sauce with hot chicken and rice.

"This recipe was one my late wife Roxanne was about to include in a cookbook she was writing just before she died."

Tonya Pinkins, formerly Livia Frye Cudahy of
ALL MY CHILDREN

African Chicken with Peanuts

MAKES 4 SERVINGS

༣༠

2 tablespoons peanut oil

6 garlic cloves, sliced

2 cups raw shelled peanuts

3½-pound chicken, cut up,
    all fat and skin removed

1 large onion, cut into chunks

Crushed red pepper

1 teaspoon salt

1 teaspoon poultry seasoning

1 teaspoon dried tarragon

1 teaspoon turmeric

½ cup tomato paste

2 chicken bouillon cubes

2 cups boiling water

1. Heat the oil in a Dutch oven or a large skillet with a tight-fitting lid.

2. Sauté the garlic in hot oil until golden, about 5 minutes.

3. Add the peanuts and stir until they are coated with oil.

4. Add the chicken, onion, and spices. Brown on all sides over high heat until the surface of the chicken is darkly browned, about 10 minutes.

5. Add the tomato paste, bouillon cubes, and boiling water. Stir, lower heat to a simmer, and cover.

6. Simmer for at least 1 hour, stirring occasionally, until the chicken falls off the bones.

7. If desired, before serving, remove the chicken pieces, put some or all of the peanut mixture into a blender, and puree it. Then stir the pureed portion back into the chicken mixture, or serve it separately as a sauce.

> *"The black population of South Africa is predominantly poor, and a staple food is 'mealie pap,' which is very similar to hominy grits boiled into a porridge. To duplicate this dish, you can simply buy hominy grits and prepare it according to the package, spooning the chicken over it. It can also be served over rice. It is excellent with cornbread or buttermilk biscuits. I like to serve citrus salad with it to cool the palate."*

Melody Thomas Scott, Nikki Abbott of
THE YOUNG AND THE RESTLESS

Melody Thomas Scott's Chicken Martiniquaise

MAKES 2 SERVINGS

4 boneless, skinless chicken
    breast halves

Salt and pepper

Flour for dusting

4 tablespoons butter

1 ounce (2 tablespoons)
    dark rum, warmed

$^1/_2$ cup heavy cream

2 small bananas, cut in half
    lengthwise

2 half-inch-thick cored
    pineapple slices

$^1/_4$ cup sugar

Peanuts

Tomato or mint leaves and
    strawberry for garnish

1. Season both sides of the chicken breasts with salt and pepper to taste.

2. Dredge the chicken in flour and shake off the excess.

3. In a large skillet, melt 2 tablespoons butter. Sauté the chicken breasts in butter until both sides are brown, about 10 minutes. Transfer the chicken to a plate and keep warm.

4. Over medium heat, add rum to the skillet and ignite. When the flame is gone, add cream and cook until thick and creamy, about 5 minutes. Taste and season with salt and pepper.

5. Return the chicken to the skillet and remove from the heat. Cover to keep warm.

6. In another large skillet, combine the remaining butter, bananas, and pineapple slices. Sauté until golden brown, about 5 minutes.

7. Sprinkle with the sugar and continue sautéing until the sugar caramelizes, about 5 minutes.

8. Place the chicken in the middle of a serving plate with the sauce on top. Garnish with pineapple. Arrange banana halves in a circle around the chicken. Top with peanuts, a tomato (cut into a rose, if you prefer), or in warmer weather, decorate with mint leaves and a strawberry.

> *"This recipe is wonderful for a romantic dinner for two at home."*

Alexia Robinson, formerly Meg Lawson of
GENERAL HOSPITAL

Alexia's Lemon Chicken Tenders

MAKES 4 SERVINGS

2 tablespoons olive oil

2 pounds chicken tenders

1/2 cup all-purpose flour

2 tablespoons butter

1/3 cup dry white wine

Juice and zest of 2 lemons

1/4 cup chopped fresh or dried parsley

1. In a large skillet, heat the oil over medium heat.

2. Dredge the chicken in flour, then sauté in hot oil until brown on both sides, about 10 minutes.

3. Add the butter, wine, lemon juice, and zest from both lemons and cook for about 5 minutes.

4. Garnish with parsley before serving.

"*This dish is great with rice or pasta. If you are diet-conscious, you can pour off the olive oil and add extra flour and a little water to thicken the sauce. Butter Buds can be substituted for real butter.*"

Sydney Penny, Julia Santos of
ALL MY CHILDREN

Chicken Cordon Bleu

MAKES 2 TO 4 SERVINGS

4 slices ham

4 slices Swiss cheese

4 boneless, skinless chicken
breast halves, pounded thin

$^1\!/_2$ cup all-purpose flour

1 egg, beaten

$^1\!/_2$ cup cornflake crumbs

6 to 8 tablespoons butter

Juice of 1 lemon or lime

3 to 4 tablespoons sour
cream

1. Place 1 ham slice and 1 cheese slice on each piece of chicken. Fold over and secure with a large toothpick.

2. Dredge in flour. Dip in egg. Roll in cornflake crumbs.

3. In a large skillet, melt 6 tablespoons butter and cook the chicken, uncovered, for 12 minutes or until cooked through. Squeeze lemon or lime juice into the skillet.

4. Transfer the chicken to a serving plate. Add remaining butter and sour cream to drippings. Stir and pour the sauce over the chicken. Serve with asparagus or green beans.

"This is a quick and wonderful dish."

Carol Lawrence, formerly Angela Eckert of
GENERAL HOSPITAL

Shrimp Scampi

MAKES 4 SERVINGS

26 to 30 large shrimp

$1/2$ cup butter

4 or 5 large garlic cloves, sliced

Large bunch of fresh parsley (preferably Italian), coarsely chopped

$1/4$ cup ice water

$1/2$ cup grated Parmesan cheese

Coarsely ground pepper

1. Shell and butterfly the shrimp, leaving the tail shell intact.

2. In a large skillet, melt the butter and sauté the garlic until golden, about 5 minutes. Remove garlic and set aside.

3. Sauté the shrimp until they are pink and firm, 5 to 10 minutes.

4. Sprinkle the parsley over the shrimp and add ice water.

5. Cover the skillet tightly; lower heat and simmer for 3 minutes.

6. Sprinkle the shrimp with cheese and pepper to taste. Cover the skillet again for 1 minute. Serve immediately with hot garlic bread.

∾

Thaao Penghlis, formerly Tony Di Mera of
DAYS OF OUR LIVES

Thaao Penghlis's Pasta and Seafood

MAKES 4 TO 6 SERVINGS

∽

³/₄ cup butter

1 medium onion, finely chopped

3 garlic cloves, finely chopped

2 dozen littleneck or cherrystone clams

¹/₂ cup all-purpose flour

1 pound sea scallops

1 pound medium shrimp, peeled

Handful of chopped fresh parsley, plus additional for serving

4 tablespoons sour cream

1 pound fresh or packaged pasta, preferably linguini

1 lemon, cut into wedges

1. In a large skillet, melt 4 tablespoons butter. Before it completely melts, add the onion and garlic. Sauté until the onion is translucent, about 5 minutes.

2. In a large pot, steam the clams in 2 cups boiling water until they open, about 10 minutes. Remove and strain the broth.

3. Add the broth to the skillet. Finely chop the clams and add to the skillet.

4. Lightly flour the scallops. Melt 4 tablespoons butter in a medium skillet and add the scallops. Cook over low heat until done, about 5 minutes. Add to the skillet with the clams.

5. Add the shrimp to the skillet with the clams and scallops. Cook 5 minutes, covered, over low heat.

6. Add the parsley and the remaining 4 tablespoons butter to the skillet.

7. Stir in the sour cream and blend well. Cook over very low heat, covered, for about 20 minutes. Keep stirring so the mixture does not stick to the pan.

8. In a large pot of boiling salted water, cook the pasta until tender, 5 minutes for fresh and 10 minutes for dried. Drain. Add the pasta to the skillet and mix with sauce.

9. Serve with parsley and lemon wedges. If desired, serve with salad and warm stuffed bread (a long, thin loaf of bread can be sliced three-quarters down and stuffed with butter and Swiss cheese; place in a 250°F. oven and warm until the cheese and butter have melted).

Brenda Brock, formerly Brenda McGillis of
ONE LIFE TO LIVE

Brother Buck's Baja Laguna Trout

MAKES 4 TO 6 SERVINGS

Olive oil

6 large skinless fillets speckled sea trout, or any other firm fish, such as snapper (36 ounces total)

Green jalapeño hot sauce

1 tablespoon chopped fresh dill

½ teaspoon salt

All-purpose flour for dusting

Lemon or lime slices

Cilantro sprigs

Pineapple Salsa Verde (recipe follows)

1. Cover the bottom of a large skillet with olive oil and warm over low heat.

2. Sprinkle or dip fillets in the jalapeño hot sauce, then dredge fillets in the dill and salt-seasoned flour.

3. Fry fillets in hot oil until golden brown on both sides, about 6 minutes.

4. Serve on warmed dishes garnished with lemon or lime and sprigs of cilantro. Accompany with Pineapple Salsa Verde.

Pineapple Salsa Verde

MAKES ABOUT 3 CUPS

1 fresh pineapple, peeled, cored, and chopped

2 Vidalia onions, or any other sweet onion

¼ cup finely chopped fresh cilantro

Juice of 2 or 3 limes

1 teaspoon sugar

Toss the ingredients together in a bowl and let sit, refrigerated for 24 hours, before serving.

"From time to time you'll find this meal featured on our specials board at Muriel's, my husband's restaurant in Newport, Rhode Island—Buen Provecho!"

Karen Lynn Gorney, formerly Tara Martin of
ALL MY CHILDREN

Auntie's Low-Fat Fish Casserole

MAKES 4 TO 6 SERVINGS

∾

6 fillets whitefish, such as sole
   or flounder (36 ounces total)

1 large onion, chopped

3 garlic cloves, chopped

Dried oregano

1 medium tomato, sliced

2 medium carrots, sliced

1 green bell pepper, cored
   and sliced

1. Preheat oven to 350°F.

2. Place fillets in the bottom of a medium baking pan.
Cover with onion and garlic. Sprinkle on oregano to taste
and add tomato, carrots, and green pepper.

3. Bake for 20 to 30 minutes, or until the fish flakes when pierced with a fork.

> "*My* Aunt Eddy, as we called her,
> was married to E. Y. Harburg, the lyricist ('Over
> the Rainbow,' 'April in Paris'). She had also been previously
> married to my dad, Jay Gorney, who wrote the music for
> 'Brother, Can You Spare a Dime?' with Mr. Harburg. We
> called her 'Aunt' because her real relationship with Dad
> was a little complicated to explain to children.
> 'She helped raise me' is an understatement.
> She was a health nut and taught me to cook and to take
> vitamins, among other lifesaving tips."

Jacklyn Zeman, Bobbie Jones of
GENERAL HOSPITAL

Sole in Tomato Sauce

MAKES 4 SERVINGS

❧

½ cup sliced fresh mushrooms

¼ cup dry white wine

1 tablespoon chopped fresh thyme, or ½ teaspoon dried

1 tablespoon tomato paste

1½ cups chopped ripe tomatoes (about 2 medium)

¼ cup chopped onion

1 garlic clove, crushed

8 thin sole fillets (about 1 pound total)

¼ teaspoon salt

1. In a large nonstick skillet, bring the mushrooms, wine, half of the fresh thyme (if using dried thyme, do not sprinkle thyme on fish fillets), the tomato paste, tomatoes, onion, and garlic to a boil; reduce heat to medium and cook, uncovered, about 10 minutes or until slightly thickened.

2. Sprinkle fish fillets with salt and remaining thyme (or dried thyme if using). Roll up and place on the tomato mixture in the skillet.

3. Cover and cook over low heat about 15 minutes, or until fish flakes easily with a fork.

"*This recipe is from* Betty Crocker's Low-Cholesterol Cookbook, *which was given to me by my mother after my daughter, Lacey Rose, was born. She bought the book for me so we could practice making a few good recipes that would help me lose weight fast. I had to return to work four weeks later. It worked! This recipe is one of our favorites. We still make it once or twice a month just because it's so good.*"

Shelley Taylor Morgan, Correspondent for E! Entertainment Television;
formerly Lorena Sharpe of GENERAL HOSPITAL

Shelley Taylor Morgan's Stroganoff for Lovers

MAKES 4 TO 6 SERVINGS

✍

2 to 3 pounds boneless round
   steak

2 pounds fresh mushrooms,
   sliced

1 large white onion, finely
   chopped

4 tablespoons butter or
   margarine

1 1/2 cups boiling water

6 beef bouillon cubes

1/2 teaspoon salt, or to taste

1/2 cup water

4 tablespoons all-purpose
   flour

1 to 1 1/2 cups sour cream

4 cups cooked rice or noodles

1. Cut the meat into thin strips.

2. In a large skillet, sauté the mushrooms and onion in the butter until the onion is translucent, about 5 minutes.

3. In a medium bowl, combine the boiling water and bouillon cubes, and pour into the skillet.

4. Add the meat, cover the skillet, and simmer for approximately 45 minutes or until the meat is tender. Season to taste with salt.

5. In a small bowl, combine the water and flour and slowly stir into the meat mixture. Cook, stirring constantly, until the mixture comes to a boil and begins to thicken.

6. Stir in the sour cream just before serving; do not let boil. Serve over rice or noodles.

"I don't eat a lot of red meat, but for special occasions I will make an exception! And in a world where everything I like is either illegal, immoral, fattening, expensive, or contributes to PMS, I think I deserve to splurge once in a while, and so should you!"

Romantic Meals

Eileen Fulton, Lisa Miller Grimaldi *of*
AS THE WORLD TURNS

Tortilla and Black or Red Bean Casserole

MAKES 6 TO 8 SERVINGS

❧

1 cup chopped onion

¾ cup chopped green bell
pepper

1 can (7½ ounces) cut-up
tomatoes (not drained)

4 garlic cloves

1 teaspoon ground cumin

⅓ cup picante sauce

1 can (16 ounces) black beans
or red beans, or ½ can each,
drained

6 to 8 corn tortillas, 5 to 6
inches in diameter

¾ cup shredded low-fat
Monterey jack cheese

¾ to 1 cup shredded lettuce

¼ cup nonfat sour cream

1 to 2 scallions, chopped

1. Preheat oven to 350°F.

2. In a large skillet, combine the onion, green pepper, tomatoes and liquid, garlic, cumin, sauce, and beans. Bring to a boil, reduce heat, and simmer uncovered for 10 minutes.

3. In a medium baking dish, spread a layer of one-third of the bean mixture, and top with 2 or 3 tortillas, overlapping if necessary. Sprinkle on half the cheese. Repeat with another layer of beans, 2 or 3 tortillas, and the remaining cheese. Complete with remaining beans and tortillas.

4. Cover and bake for 25 to 30 minutes or until bubbling. Let stand for 10 minutes.

5. Top with shredded lettuce, scallions, and dollops of sour cream. Cut into squares and serve.

"It is nourishing, delicious, low in fat, and high in energy. Plus it's pretty!"

Kimberlin Brown, Sheila Carter Forrester of
THE BOLD AND THE BEAUTIFUL

Pinto Beans Portuguese Style

MAKES 6 TO 8 SERVINGS

1 pound dried pinto beans

1 tablespoon baking soda

3 large onions, chopped

1/2 cup chopped salt pork

1 cup chopped green bell pepper

1 garlic clove, chopped

1 can (8 ounces) Italian-style marinara sauce

1/3 cup catsup

1/2 cup white vinegar

2 teaspoons salt

1/4 teaspoon black pepper

1/2 teaspoon ground cumin

1/4 teaspoon ground cinnamon

1. Rinse the beans in a colander.

2. In a large bowl, combine the beans and enough warm water to cover them by 2 inches. Add the baking soda and soak overnight.

3. In the morning, rinse the beans and transfer to a large pot of water. Bring to a boil and cook for 3 minutes. Drain in a colander and rinse with cold water.

4. Place the beans back in the pot. Add onions, salt pork, green pepper, and garlic. Add cold water enough to cover the contents to the pot and bring to a boil. Cover and simmer for 1 hour or until the beans are tender.

5. Stir in the marinara sauce, catsup, vinegar, salt, pepper, cumin, and cinnamon. Simmer an additional hour. (For thicker beans, transfer the mixture, after simmering, to a covered casserole dish and bake in a 350°F. oven for 30 minutes.) Serve.

∽

Margaret Reed, *formerly Shannon O'Hara McKechnie of*
AS THE WORLD TURNS

Spinach and Rice Gratin

MAKES 4 TO 6 SERVINGS

❧

2 pounds fresh spinach,
    washed and stemmed;
    or 2 packages
    (10 ounces each)
    frozen, thawed

1 tablespoon butter or
    safflower oil

$1/2$ medium onion, minced

$1/2$ teaspoon dried thyme
    or rosemary, or a combination

Pinch of grated nutmeg

$1^1/2$ cups cooked brown rice
    ($1/2$ cup raw)

1 cup grated Swiss or
    mozzarella cheese

$1/4$ cup grated Parmesan cheese

Salt and ground pepper

2 tablespoons whole wheat
    bread crumbs

1. Preheat oven to 350°F. Butter a medium casserole.

2. If using fresh spinach, blanch, squeeze dry, and chop fine. If using thawed frozen, squeeze dry and chop.

3. Heat the butter in a large heavy-bottomed skillet and sauté the onion until translucent, about 5 minutes. Add the spinach and toss for 1 to 2 minutes.

4. Add the thyme and/or rosemary and nutmeg and remove from the heat.

5. Toss with the rice and cheeses, and add salt and pepper to taste.

6. Transfer the mixture to the prepared casserole and sprinkle the bread crumbs over the top. Bake for 30 minutes or until bubbly.

❧

Carol Lawrence, formerly Angela Eckert of
GENERAL HOSPITAL

Pasta e Fagioli

MAKES 4 SERVINGS

❧

1 large yellow onion, chopped

2 tablespoons canola or virgin olive oil

1 can (8 ounces) tomato paste

Salt and pepper

Chopped fresh parsley

Chopped fresh basil

1 can (16 ounces) kidney beans or cannellini beans

½ pound pasta shells

Grated Parmesan cheese

1. In a medium skillet, sauté the onion in oil until translucent, about 5 minutes.

2. Add the tomato paste, salt and pepper, parsley, and basil and simmer for 10 minutes. Add the strained beans and simmer for 5 more minutes.

3. In a medium pot of lightly salted water, boil the shells until tender, about 10 minutes. Drain and return to the pan.

4. Add the tomato mixture to the shells, divide into serving portions, and sprinkle each serving with grated Parmesan cheese.

∾

James Kiberd, Trevor Dillon of
ALL MY CHILDREN

Pasta con Tonno alla Trevor

MAKES 4 TO 6 SERVINGS

1 pound whole wheat linguine

2 tablespoons olive oil

3 medium onions, sliced stem to top

1 can (7 ounces) tuna packed in water, flaked

1 can (15½ ounces) chickpeas with juice

10 to 12 small pitted olives, drained

Chopped fresh parsley for garnish

Black pepper

1. In a large pot of lightly salted boiling water, cook the pasta until al dente, about 10 minutes. Drain.

2. In a medium skillet, heat the olive oil and sauté the onions until translucent, about 5 minutes.

3. Add the tuna with water, chickpeas with juice, and olives. Simmer for 5 minutes.

4. Toss the tuna mixture with the pasta and garnish with parsley; add pepper to taste. Serve with a fresh green salad.

> "*I learned this recipe from an Italian friend who was a chef. A group of friends from around the world were staying at a farmhouse in the hills outside of Florence, and we needed tasty, healthy, inexpensive meals to prepare. This was a favorite. Once you make it you never forget it. And you can take it wherever you go!*"

Julia Barr, Brooke English of
ALL MY CHILDREN

Allison's Vegetable Pasta Salad

MAKES 4 SERVINGS

෴

1 package (12 ounces)
  fettuccine

3 cups broccoli florets

$1/3$ cup olive oil

1 teaspoon salt

$1/2$ medium onion, chopped

3 garlic cloves, minced

2 tablespoons chopped
  fresh basil

1 pint cherry tomatoes, cut
  in half

$1/2$ teaspoon ground black
  pepper

$1/2$ teaspoon crushed red
  pepper (optional)

$1/2$ cup grated Parmesan
  cheese

1. In a large pot of lightly salted boiling water, cook the fettuccine until tender, about 10 minutes.

2. While the pasta is cooking, blanch the broccoli in boiling water for 2 minutes, until bright green but still crisp; drain and rinse in cold water.

3. Drain the fettuccine and place in a serving bowl. Toss the pasta with 1 tablespoon olive oil and $1/2$ teaspoon salt; set aside.

4. In a large skillet, heat the remaining oil. Add the onion and sauté until translucent, about 5 minutes. Add the garlic and basil, and cook briefly, about 1 minute. Add the tomatoes and cook about 2 minutes. Sprinkle with the remaining $1/2$ teaspoon salt and the black pepper.

5. Remove pan from the heat and let the mixture cool, about 5 minutes.

6. Gently stir in the cooked broccoli and crushed red pepper. Add the vegetable mixture to the pasta. Add 2 tablespoons of the cheese and toss. Save the remaining cheese to serve over the pasta.

❧

Kimberlin Brown, Sheila Carter Forrester of
THE BOLD AND THE BEAUTIFUL

Kimberlin Brown's Famous Pesto

MAKES 4 TO 6 SERVINGS

2 cups fresh basil leaves

1/2 cup fresh parsley leaves

1 1/2 to 2 cups pine nuts

1/2 cup grated Parmesan cheese

1/2 cup grated Romano cheese

1/2 teaspoon salt

1/2 teaspoon pepper

2 or 3 garlic cloves (optional), minced

3 tablespoons butter or margarine

1 cup olive oil

1. In a food processor, chop basil, parsley, and pine nuts

extra-fine. (If pine nuts are not available, you can use walnuts or almonds.)

2. Mix in all the other ingredients, saving the olive oil for last, then mix the oil in a little at a time until the desired thickness.

3. Add a little pasta cooking water to the pesto before serving to thin to desired consistency.

> "*I love this recipe because it's simple and flexible. Pesto is easy to make and can be served on chicken, beef, and fish as well as pasta. And since it tastes a little different with each base, it can be served a lot.*"

Patricia Elliott, Renée Buchanan of
ONE LIFE TO LIVE

Hijiki Heaven

MAKES 8 TO 10 SERVINGS

1 to 2 ounces loose hijiki or
½ to 1 package
(2 to 4 ounces)*

½ cup sesame seeds

2 tablespoons Asian sesame oil

Juice of 1 lemon

2 cups apple juice

*1 tablespoon tamari, or more
to taste*

*1 cup fresh bulk (not
packaged) raisins*

1. In a large pot of water, soak the loose hijiki for at least 15 minutes. (It expands quite a bit, so give it lots of space.) The purpose of soaking the hijiki is to remove the salty taste and to prepare it for cooking. Drain.

*Hijiki (*he-jee-kee*) is a spaghetti-shaped seaweed that has a delectable toughness to it, a little like bacon. Note: For this recipe you can also use another, less expensive seaweed called Arame (*ah-rah-meh*), which is more leafy in texture.

2. In a large frying pan, sauté the sesame seeds in $1/2$ table-spoon sesame oil. When they start to brown a little, add the hijiki. Continue to sauté over medium heat for at least 10 minutes, turning the hijiki often and letting it become browned and a little crispy.

3. Stir in the lemon juice. Add the apple juice, tamari, and raisins. Stir and cover tightly. Simmer for at least 30 minutes, turning it often. (Don't overcook this dish.) Toss with remaining sesame oil. Serve hot, reheated, or cold. This dish also tastes wonderful stirred into brown rice.

> *"I promise you this is a delicious and adventuresome dish, and whenever I am invited to a potluck supper I bring it along. It's always a huge success, and I am asked over and over again for the recipe. It is fabulous cold by itself or in a summer salad."*

a
Gathering
of Suspects

∾

Comfort Foods for Any Occasion

At least twice a year it's mandatory on soaps to gather all the characters together for an occasion, such as a wedding. This plot device kicks off a major storyline, usually a murder mystery where everyone in the room is a suspect. But regardless of the story, the group still has to be fed. "A Gathering of Suspects" provides us with a collection of surefire comfort recipes that are perfect for parties or other occasions.

Kate Linder, Esther Valentine of
THE YOUNG AND THE RESTLESS

Kate Linder's Pumpkin Bread

MAKES THREE 1-POUND LOAVES

෨

3$^{1}/_{2}$ cups all-purpose flour

3 cups sugar

2 teaspoons baking soda

1 teaspoon ground cinnamon

1 teaspoon grated nutmeg

1$^{1}/_{2}$ teaspoons salt

4 eggs, beaten

1 cup oil

$^{2}/_{3}$ cup water

2 cups cooked and mashed pumpkin

1. Preheat oven to 350°F. Lightly grease three 9 x 5-inch loaf pans.

2. In a large bowl, sift together the flour, sugar, baking soda, cinnamon, nutmeg, and salt.

3. In another large bowl, combine the eggs, oil, water, and pumpkin and mix well. Stir into the dry ingredients.

4. Pour mixture into the loaf pans and bake for 1 hour, or until a cake tester inserted in the center comes out clean.

5. Cool before slicing.

> "*This bread comes out right every time. It's a foolproof gift from your kitchen.*"

A Gathering of Suspects

Lauren-Marie Taylor, formerly Stacey Forbes of
LOVING

Katie's Corn Muffins

MAKES 10 MUFFINS

❧

1¼ cups yellow cornmeal

1 cup all-purpose flour

¼ cup sugar

½ teaspoon salt

1 tablespoon baking powder

Pinch of black pepper

½ cup butter or margarine, softened

½ cup frozen corn kernels, thawed

1 cup half-and-half

1 egg

Dash of Tabasco sauce (optional)

1. Preheat oven to 400°F.

2. With a fork, stir together the cornmeal, flour, sugar, salt, baking powder, and pepper in a large bowl.

3. Using 2 knives, cut in the butter until it is crumbly. Add corn.

4. In a separate bowl, mix the half-and-half, egg, and Tabasco sauce, if desired. Add to the flour and corn mixture.

5. Grease 10 muffin tins and spoon the mixture into each, filling just about to the top.

6. Bake for 25 minutes only; don't let muffins get too brown on top. Serve with butter or honey.

> *"This is just one of many easy recipes that are enjoyed by my children—they not only gobble these muffins down on Saturday mornings but they also help to make them. (It beats TV!) We use standard muffin tins as well as bite-size tins, which you can find in the bakeware section of the supermarket. Easy on the pepper if they are just for kids. Adults love these with chili!"*

Mark Pinter, Grant Harrison of
ANOTHER WORLD

Mark Pinter's Hiccup–Hot Red Pepper Jelly

MAKES SEVEN 8-OUNCE JARS

∞

2 cups fresh hot peppers
   (serranos, jalapeños, or
   a mix), washed, stemmed
   (but not seeded), and
   finely chopped
½ cup finely chopped
   red bell pepper

1½ cups cider vinegar

1 teaspoon salt

6½ cups sugar

1 package (6 ounces) liquid
   pectin

1. Sterilize seven 8-ounce jelly jars according to directions that come with the jars.

2. Place pepper, vinegar, and salt in a pot. Bring the mixture to a boil and simmer for 5 minutes, stirring occasionally.

3. Add water, if needed, so the total mixture is 3 cups. Stir in the sugar. Bring to a rolling boil, and boil for 1 minute. Add the pectin while boiling and boil for 1 minute more, stirring occasionally. Remove from heat.

4. Ladle into sterilized jars, leaving about $1/4$ inch at the top. Seal jars, process in hot-water bath according to jar manufacturer's instructions, and allow to cool.

~

James Reynolds, Abe Carver of
DAYS OF OUR LIVES

James Reynolds's Spicy Apple Sausage Dressing

MAKES 6 TO 8 SERVINGS

᠅

6 tart green apples, such as
    Pippins or Granny Smiths

2 large white onions

5 or 6 celery stalks

1 cup butter

2 loaves bread (whole wheat,
    white, or egg)

6 hot Italian sausages, skins
    removed and meat crumbled
    and browned lightly

1 tablespoon rubbed dry sage

Tabasco sauce

Salt and pepper

1. Preheat oven to 350°F.

2. Chop the apples, onions, and celery.

3. In a large skillet, sauté the onions in $1/2$ cup butter until translucent, about 5 minutes.

4. In a large bowl, crumble the bread. Add the sausage and sage. Melt the remaining butter and stir in.

5. Add the bread mixture to the skillet and stir. Add a liberal dash of Tabasco or to taste. Season with salt and pepper to taste.

6. Place the stuffing in a medium baking dish and bake until lightly browned, approximately 20 minutes.

A Gathering of Suspects

Kate Linder, Esther Valentine of
THE YOUNG AND THE RESTLESS

Kate Linder's Thanksgiving Sweet Potato Eggnog Pudding

MAKES 10 TO 12 SERVINGS

∾

2 cans (8 ounces each) sweet potatoes, or 3 to 4 medium sweet potatoes, cooked

2 tablespoons butter, melted

1 cup eggnog

3/4 cup sugar

1/2 teaspoon salt

1/2 teaspoon ground cinnamon

1/2 teaspoon ground ginger

2 tablespoons grated orange rind

1/2 cup finely chopped walnuts

1. Preheat oven to 375°F. Grease a 1½-quart baking dish.

Love and Dishes

2. In a large bowl, beat the sweet potatoes with a rotary beater until thoroughly mashed. Add the butter, eggnog, sugar, salt, cinnamon, and ginger. Beat until fluffy and well blended.

3. Fold in the orange rind and walnuts.

4. Pour the mixture into a prepared baking dish.

5. Bake for 40 minutes or until the surface is golden.

"My mom made this for years and now we both make it every year. It's delicious and I'm glad that I finally got the recipe."

Patricia Elliott, Renée Buchanan of
ONE LIFE TO LIVE

Sweet Potato Oranges

SERVINGS PROPORTIONATE TO NUMBER OF DINERS

⁐

2 small sweet potatoes
  per person
2 large oranges per person
Fresh lemon juice
Apple juice
Ground cinnamon

Heavy cream
Marshmallows, chocolate
  kisses, candy-coated
  chocolate pieces, carob
  chips, or raisins for
  topping

1. This dish is best made the night before. In a large pot of salted boiling water, cook the sweet potatoes until tender when pierced with the tip of a knife, 20 to 35 minutes, depending on size. Drain, rinse under cold water, and cool until tepid. Peel and mash until smooth. Place in a large bowl.

2. While the potatoes are cooking, scrub and wash the oranges in a solution of cider vinegar and a drop of liquid soap to clean off any pesticides. On the stem end of the oranges, cut an opening about $1^{1}/_{2}$ inches in diameter. Using a serrated knife, core and clean the insides of the oranges.

3. Fold a little lemon juice, some apple juice, and cinnamon to taste into the sweet potatoes. Slowly add some cream, being careful to keep the potatoes fluffy. (Too much liquid and the cream will make the potatoes heavy and soggy.)

4. Fill each orange with $1/3$ cup of the sweet potato mixture. Place the oranges in a baking pan and cover with plastic wrap. Refrigerate overnight. About 2 hours before serving, remove the baking pan from the refrigerator and warm to room temperature.

5. About 1 hour before serving, preheat the oven to 325°F. According to your taste, top each of the oranges with either marshmallows, chocolate kisses, chocolate pieces, carob chips, or raisins. Heat the orange enough to melt the topping, about 10 minutes.

> "*This is a colorful, scrumptious, and unique way to make a Thanksgiving favorite. I have served this year after year, and it is always the most popular item of the meal. It's decorative for your table, smells delicious, and tastes even better. The secret is the orange taste, which permeates the sweet potato and enhances its already delicious flavor.*"

Linda Cook, *formerly Egypt Masters of*
LOVING

Grandma Sadie Stone Cook's West Texas Sweetheart Salad

MAKES 6 TO 8 SERVINGS

෴

1 package (8 ounces)
cream cheese, softened

1 jar (8 to 10 ounces)
maraschino cherries, chopped
(retain juice and save
1 cherry for garnish)

1 package (6 ounces) lemon
gelatin

2 cups boiling water

1 can (8¼ ounces) crushed
pineapple

1 pint heavy cream

Sugar

½ teaspoon vanilla extract

1. In a large bowl, mash the cream cheese with a fork until smooth.

2. Pour the cherry juice into a 2-cup measuring cup. Add ice water until you have a total of $1^1/4$ cups liquid. Add to the cream cheese.

3. Put the gelatin in a small bowl; add boiling water, and stir until dissolved. Add the hot mixture to the cream cheese and stir with a fork until the lumps are small.

4. Stir in the pineapple and chopped cherries.

5. Transfer the bowl to the refrigerator and cool until partly set, 4 to 5 hours.

6. Remove the bowl from the refrigerator. Whip cream until stiff, then add sugar to taste and vanilla. Fold cream into gelatin mixture until blended.

7. Pour into a large crystal serving dish. Refrigerate until set, about 1 hour. Add cherry garnish before serving.

"This pretty pink salad is delicious served on the main plate with holiday turkey or duck. Not only a family favorite, it is much in demand with my friends in New York, for their buffet parties."

Lauralee Bell, Christine Romalotti of
THE YOUNG AND THE RESTLESS

Lauralee Bell's Egg Surprise

MAKES 4 TO 6 SERVINGS

❧

$^1/_2$ *cup shredded cheddar cheese*

4 tablespoons butter, in pieces

$2^3/_4$ *cups skim milk*

8 slices whole grain bread, crusts removed

4 eggs

1. Mix the cheese, butter, and $^1/_4$ cup skim milk in a blender and set aside.

2. Cut the bread slices into quarters and spread the cheese mixture on both sides of each quarter-slice. Stack the bread quarters in a casserole dish.

3. Beat together the eggs and the remaining 2¹/₂ cups milk. Pour the egg mixture over the bread quarters.

4. Place the casserole in the refrigerator overnight.

5. One hour before serving, preheat the oven to 225°F. Place the casserole in the oven and bake for 1 hour or until brown and crispy.

> *"This has been a holiday and Sunday brunch recipe in the Bell household for years."*

Tommy Michaels, Timmy Hunter of
ALL MY CHILDREN

Tomato-Tuna Cheese Melt

MAKES 1 OR 2 SERVINGS

❧

1 can (7 ounces) tuna, drained

2 tablespoons mayonnaise, or to taste

2 slices white bread

2 slices large ripe tomato

2 slices American cheese

1. In a small bowl, mix the tuna with mayonnaise. (Chopped or minced celery can be added, too.)

2. Lightly toast the bread and spread tuna on each slice.

3. Top with a tomato slice and a cheese slice.

4. Put in the toaster oven on a piece of aluminum foil to prevent the cheese from dripping onto the tray. Broil until cheese melts, 1 to 2 minutes.

> *"I like to make this because it sure beats the plain old tuna sandwich. My friends think it's cool, too, that I 'cook.'"*

Wortham Krimmer, Andrew Carpenter of
ONE LIFE TO LIVE

Cornbread
MAKES 6 TO 8 SERVINGS

∽

$^1/_2$ cup butter, softened

1 can (8 ounces) corn, drained

1 can (8 ounces) creamed corn

2 eggs, lightly beaten

1 package (8.5 ounces)
  corn muffin mix

1. Preheat oven to 350° F.

2. In a large bowl, combine all ingredients until blended, but don't beat.

3. Pour into greased and floured loaf pan.

4. Bake for 1 hour, or until the top is lightly browned.

" It's the creamed corn that makes the difference."

Cliffhangers

❧

Desserts

It's Friday, and the soaps are over. Friday—the worst cliffhanger day of the week. Friday—the day we know that tomorrow there will be no story. And Sunday there will be no story. Friday—the day we'll have to wait until Monday to find out whether our leading lady's evil twin sister arrived in town, or the antihero will regain control of his megacorporation, or our star-crossed lovers have reunited—for the fourth time. But don't worry, there's comfort ahead. What's a major meal without a dynamic dessert? The answer is nothing, or at least not enough. So we have included the sweetest dessert recipes we could find.

Martha Byrne, Lily Grimaldi of
AS THE WORLD TURNS

Chocolate Icebox Cake

MAKES 8 TO 10 SERVINGS

$1/2$ pound sweet cooking
    chocolate

3 tablespoons water

2 egg yolks

2 tablespoons confectioners'
    sugar

1 cup heavy cream

2 egg whites, stiffly beaten

12 double ladyfingers, or 24
    strips sponge cake

1. Melt the chocolate in a double boiler. Add water and blend.

2. Transfer the chocolate to a large bowl. Add egg yolks to the chocolate, and beat vigorously until smooth. Add the sugar and mix well. Whip the cream until stiff and fold into the chocolate mixture. Fold in egg whites.

3. Separate ladyfingers. Line an 8 x 4-inch loaf pan with waxed paper. Line the bottom with single ladyfingers; cut the remaining ladyfingers in half crosswise and use to line the sides of the pan.

4. Fill pan with chocolate mixture. Chill 12 to 24 hours.

5. Unmold chocolate cake. Serve with additional whipped cream or with whipped dessert topping mix, if desired.

Optional: For a really special occasion, make this cake in a heart-shaped pan and garnish with raspberries or other fresh fruit.

∽

Chris Robinson, *formerly Jack Hamilton of*
THE BOLD AND THE BEAUTIFUL

Chocolate Chip Bread

MAKES TWO 8-INCH LOAVES

1 package active dry yeast

3 cups all-purpose flour

2 tablespoons brown sugar

2 tablespoons granulated sugar

1 teaspoon salt

1 teaspoon ground cinnamon

4 tablespoons butter, melted

1 egg

1 cup milk

¼ cup water

1 cup chocolate chips

If you use a bread machine

Pour the first 10 ingredients in the order listed into the pan, select White Bread, and push Start. Five minutes from the end of the second mixing, add the chocolate chips. Follow instructions beginning with Step 3.

To prepare on the stove top

1. Heat the water and milk in a medium saucepan, until just tepid (90 to 100°F.).

2. Transfer to a large bowl and stir in the yeast, butter, salt, and sugars. Stir until the mixture is evenly mixed. Slowly stir in the flour and add the other ingredients. Turn the dough out onto a well-floured work surface and knead for at least 10 minutes, adding more flour as needed, until the dough is smooth and elastic.

3. Lightly grease a large bowl. Place the ball of dough in the bowl and turn to coat evenly with grease. Cover with plastic wrap and let rise in a draft-free place, until loaf is about one and a half times its original volume, about 2 hours. (When the dough has risen enough, a finger inserted 1/2 inch into the dough will leave an impression.)

4. Cut the dough into 2 portions and shape into loaves. Transfer each loaf to a greased 8 x 4-inch loaf pan. Cover the pans with plastic wrap and let stand in a draft-free place until the dough is one and a half times its original volume, about 1 hour.

5. Preheat oven to 350°F. Place loaf pans in oven and bake until brown, 40 to 45 minutes. Allow loaves to cool completely on a wire rack before serving.

> *"It is just like eating a chocolate chip cookie. It tastes great, and it's beautiful to look at!"*

Russell Todd, Jerry Birn of
THE BOLD AND THE BEAUTIFUL

Cranberry Apple Delight

MAKES 6 TO 8 SERVINGS

∾

2 cups fresh cranberries

3 cups sliced apples

½ cup raisins

1 tablespoon lemon juice

¼ teaspoon salt

1 cup packed brown sugar

½ cup granulated sugar

1 cup quick-cooking oats

½ cup all-purpose flour

⅓ cup margarine, softened

1. Preheat oven to 325°F.

2. In a large bowl, combine the cranberries, apples, raisins, lemon juice, and salt. Transfer the mixture to a greased 13 x 9-inch baking dish.

3. In a large bowl, combine the remaining ingredients. Place on top of the first mixture.

4. Bake for 1 hour or until the topping is slightly brown. This can be served warm or cold.

> *"This is a great dessert recipe, especially around Thanksgiving. It's my favorite because it combines the great tastes of cranberries and apples. Best of all, it's easy and quick. In my home it never makes it to day two."*

Rebecca Holden, *formerly Elena Parsons of*
GENERAL HOSPITAL

Banana Split Pie

MAKES 8 SERVINGS

❧

2 cups graham cracker crumbs

¹/₂ cup butter

2 cups sugar

2 packages (8 ounces each)
cream cheese

4 large bananas, sliced

1 can (20 ounces) crushed
pineapple, drained

1 large container whipped
topping

¹/₄ cup each graham cracker
crumbs, chopped walnuts
or pecans, and sliced
strawberries or cherries

1. Preheat oven to 350°F. Mix the graham cracker crumbs
and butter and press into a 13 x 9-inch pan.

2. Bake the crust for 5 minutes. Blend the sugar and cream
cheese and spread over the crust.

3. Place the banana slices over the filling and spread the pineapple over the bananas. Top with the whipped topping.

4. Sprinkle the 1/4 cup graham cracker crumbs and chopped walnuts or pecans over the whipped topping. Garnish with strawberries or cherries.

> *"I've taken this to numerous church socials and potluck suppers and always get rave reviews and lots of requests for the recipe."*

Kristina Wagner, Felicia Jones of
GENERAL HOSPITAL

Aunt Carolyn's Pumpkin Pie

MAKES 8 SERVINGS

᠃᠊ᢀ

Top Crust

1 1/2 cups all-purpose flour

1/2 teaspoon salt

1 teaspoon baking powder

1/2 cup vegetable shortening

1/4 cup ice water

Filling

1 1/2 cups pumpkin puree

1/2 cup brown sugar

1/2 cup granulated sugar

1 teaspoon ground
   cinnamon

1/4 teaspoon ground cloves

1/4 teaspoon ground ginger

2 eggs, lightly beaten

1 cup milk

1 unbaked 9-inch pie shell

1. Prepare top crust: In a medium bowl, combine flour, salt, and baking powder. Using a pastry blender or 2 knives, cut in the shortening until the mixture resembles coarse meal. Tossing the mixture with a fork, gradually sprinkle in the ice water until just moistened and the dough holds together when pinched between your thumb and forefinger. Gather up the dough and knead it once or twice. Cut into 2 portions. (As you are only using one portion for this pie, the other portion can be wrapped in waxed paper—pat margarine around the pastry—and kept in the refrigerator for a few days.)

2. On a lightly floured work surface, using a lightly floured rolling pin, roll out the dough into a 10-inch circle about $1/8$ inch thick. Preheat oven to 425°F.

3. Prepare filling: In a large bowl, mix the pumpkin and dry ingredients thoroughly. Add the eggs and milk. Pour into the pie shell. Carefully transfer the top crust over the filling. Press the edges of the crusts together to seal. Roll up the excess dough around the edges to form a thick rope and flute it. Cut a 2-inch slash in the top crust. Lightly brush the top of the pie with some milk.

4. Bake for 45 to 50 minutes, or until a knife inserted in the center of the pie comes out clean.

"*Don't even think about any other pumpkin pie recipe.*"

Cliffhangers

Judith McConnell, formerly Sophia Capwell of
SANTA BARBARA

Aimee's (my Grandmother) Apple Pie

MAKES 8 SERVINGS

Crust

3 cups all-purpose flour

$^1\!/_4$ cup sugar

Pinch of salt

$^1\!/_2$ cup butter, chilled and cut into $^1\!/_2$-inch cubes

$^1\!/_3$ cup vegetable shortening, chilled

$^1\!/_2$ cup cold water

Filling

7 to 9 Granny Smith apples, peeled, cored, and cut into $^1\!/_2$-inch-thick slices

Juice of 1 lemon

Butter

Sugar

Ground cinnamon

1 teaspoon cornstarch

Milk

1. Prepare the dough: in a medium bowl, combine the flour, sugar, and salt and toss well to blend. Using a pastry blender or 2 knives, cut in the butter and shortening until the mixture resembles coarse meal. Tossing the mixture with a fork, gradually sprinkle in the ice water, 2 tablespoons at a time, until just moistened and the dough holds together when pinched between your thumb and forefinger. (If needed, add more ice water, 1 tablespoon at a time.) Gather up the dough and knead it once or twice. Cut into 2 pieces in one-third and two-thirds proportions. Press each into a thick flat disk, wrap in waxed paper, and refrigerate for 45 minutes.

2. Preheat oven to 450°F.

3. In a large bowl, toss together the apples and lemon juice. On a lightly floured work surface, using a lightly floured rolling pin, roll out the larger portion of dough into a 12-inch circle about $1/8$ inch thick. Gently transfer the dough to a 9-inch pie pan. Layer in the apples and dot with butter. Sprinkle some sugar, cinnamon, and cornstarch over. Continue to layer and add sugar, cinnamon, and cornstarch until apples have filled the pan and are slightly mounded.

4. Roll out the smaller portion of dough into a 10-inch circle about $1/8$ inch thick, and place over the apples. Press the edges of the crusts together to seal. Roll up the dough around the edges to form a thick rope and flute it. Cut a 2-inch slash in the top crust. Lightly brush with some milk.

5. Bake for 10 minutes. Reduce heat to 350°F. and bake until the crust is golden brown, 35 to 45 minutes. Serve warm with sharp cheese or ice cream.

Cliffhangers

Kimberlin Brown, Sheila Carter Forrester of
THE BOLD AND THE BEAUTIFUL

Kimberlin Brown's Peaches and Cream Pie

MAKES 8 SERVINGS

2 cans (16 ounces each) sliced peaches

1 egg

3/4 cup heavy cream

2 tablespoons all-purpose flour

1/3 cup sugar

1/2 teaspoon salt

1/2 teaspoon grated nutmeg

1/4 teaspoon ground cinnamon

Store-bought dough for double-crust pie

1. Preheat oven to 375°F.

2. Drain the peaches and cut any large slices in half lengthwise.

3. In a medium bowl, combine the remaining ingredients except the crust. Beat with a wire whip or rotary beater until smooth.

4. Cut the dough into 2 pieces. On a lightly floured work surface, using a lightly floured rolling pin, roll out one portion of dough into a 12-inch circle about $1/8$ inch thick. Gently transfer to a 9-inch pie plate. Arrange drained peaches evenly in the pie crust. Pour the cream mixture over the peaches.

5. Roll out the remaining portion of the dough into a 10-inch circle about $1/8$ inch thick, and place over the filling. Press the edges together to seal. Roll up the excess dough around the edges to form a thick rope and flute it. Cut a 2-inch slash in the top crust.

6. Cover the edge with foil. Bake for 25 minutes. Remove foil and bake 20 to 25 minutes longer, until crust is golden brown. Refrigerate until ready to serve.

Variation: Creamy Apple Pie

Substitute 4 cups sliced, peeled apples (about 2 pounds) for canned peaches and increase sugar to $2/3$ cup. Increase baking time 5 to 10 minutes.

> *"I love to cook things that are easy and not at all time-consuming, but that taste as though you spent the afternoon slaving away over the stove. This is one of those recipes. I often make this pie for romantic evenings and special occasions and it's always a hit."*

Cliffhangers

Elvera Roussel, formerly Hope Bauer Spaulding of
GUIDING LIGHT

Aunt Irma's Kugel (Noodle Pudding)

MAKES 6 TO 8 SERVINGS

1 pound wide egg noodles

6 eggs

1 pint sour cream

1¼ cups sugar

¾ pound cream cheese, softened

1 cup butter, plus 4 tablespoons melted butter

Canned peaches or pineapple, drained (optional)

1½ cups cornflake crumbs

1. Grease a large baking pan.

2. In a large pot of lightly salted water, boil the noodles until tender, about 9 minutes. Drain.

3. In a large bowl, beat the eggs. Add the sour cream and 1 cup sugar. Add the cream cheese and 1 cup butter and mix thoroughly. Stir in the canned fruit, if using.

4. Mix in the noodles. In a separate bowl, mix the melted butter and cornflake crumbs.

5. Pour the mixture into a baking pan. Sprinkle the topping mixture evenly over the top of the noodles. Cover the pan with plastic wrap and set in the refrigerator for several hours or overnight.

6. The next day, preheat oven to 325°F. Bake 1 to $1^1/2$ hours or until slightly browned.

∞

Thom Christopher, formerly Dante Partou of
LOVING

Jelled Café Creevey

MAKES 4 SERVINGS

༄

2 cups cold, very strong coffee
1 envelope unflavored gelatin
¼ cup sugar
¼ cup brandy

Heavy cream, whipped to
soft peaks
Sweet chocolate shavings

1. In a large saucepan, heat the coffee with gelatin.

2. Add the sugar. Stir until gelatin and sugar are dissolved: Do not bring to a boil.

3. Remove the saucepan from the heat to cool for 5 to 10 minutes. Stir in the brandy.

4. Pour the mixture into dessert glasses; chill until firm, about 1 hour. Top with whipped cream and chocolate shavings.

Contributors' Profiles

Julia Barr

An Emmy Award winner (as Outstanding Supporting Actress) for her popular *All My Children* character, Brooke English, Julia Barr was born and raised in Indiana.

As a teenager she decided to forgo "hanging out" with her pals to work with the Fort Wayne Community Theater. While at Purdue University she appeared in college productions of *Endgame, A Streetcar Named Desire,* and *Our Town.* Early professional credits include *Scapino* and *Never Too Late.* On TV she was cast as Charles Adams's daughter in *The Adams Chronicles* on PBS.

After a five-month stint on *Ryan's Hope* as Reenie Szabo, Barr joined *AMC* toward the late 1970s. In 1981 she left the series for fifteen months and toured in the stage play *West Side Waltz,* with Katharine Hepburn and Dorothy Loudon. (She returned to *AMC* in 1983.)

Barr and her husband, oral surgeon Richard Hirschlag, have an eleven-year-old daughter, Allison.

∽

Lauralee Bell

When Lauralee Bell (Christine "Cricket" Blair Romalotti, *The Young and the Restless)* was nine years old, she asked her parents if she could be a nonspeaking extra on *Y&R.* Since her folks, William Bell and Lee Phillip Bell, are executive producers of the series, permission wasn't too hard to come by. Although she continued to make appearances during school vacations over the next few years, she couldn't rely on "family connections" for permanent work; she never knew after each appearance if she would be asked back. But by the time Bell was thirteen, her character, Cricket, a teenage model, was so popular with viewers that the role was expanded from recurring to contract. (A recurring character shows up once or twice a month; the actor has not signed a contract with the show.) Cricket, now in her early twenties, is an attorney.

When the family moved to L.A., Bell became a contract player. She finished her senior year of high school on the West Coast, and returned to Chicago to accept her diploma with her classmates at the Latin School.

Bell, whose two older brothers, William Bell, Jr., and Bradley, are also members of the "family firm," enjoys tennis.

∽

Brenda Brock

Brenda Brock (who portrayed Brenda McGillis on *One Life to Live*) was born in Beaumont, Texas, and raised outside Dallas. She attended the University of Texas at Austin as a nursing major, but later switched to the drama department when she won a scholarship.

Before her final semester, Brock took a break from school and was a cook for a geology research project looking for uranium on the border of Mexico. When the project was completed, Brock moved to Denver, where she spent two years at the Denver Center Theater Company. Her credits with DCTC include *The Hostage, Arms and the Man,* and *The Taming of the Shrew.*

An accomplished playwright, Brock has completed *Summer at Pilares* and is putting the finishing touches on *Wailing Wives,* a drama about the women left behind by nineteenth-century New England whalers.

Brock lives in Rhode Island with her husband, Paul Barclay de la Tolley, and their daughter, Lela. The couple are actively involved in the running of their family-owned restaurant, Muriel's.

෴

Contributors' Profiles

Kimberlin Brown

As a little girl who preferred Lincoln Logs to Barbie dolls, Kimberlin Brown (Sheila Carter Forrester, *The Bold and the Beautiful*) knew she wanted to be an architect. (While still in high school, she had a job drafting floor plans for a carpet company.) Her career plans changed when her high school friends encouraged her to enter a beauty contest. Brown won the Miss Le Mesa (California) Pageant, and was later the first runner-up in the Miss California USA Pageant. One of the judges—model agent Nina Blanchard—approached Brown about modeling, a career opportunity Brown initially (albeit politely) turned down. She eventually changed her mind and was soon modeling in Tokyo, Milan, and Paris.

Blanchard later sent Brown on casting calls for TV series and films; among Brown's credits are *Matt Houston, Eye of the Tiger, 18 Again,* and *Who's That Girl.* In May 1990 Brown was cast as evil nurse Sheila Carter on *The Young and the Restless.* Two years later, the character was "crossed over" to *Y&R*'s sister soap, where she continues to create havoc.

Brown is married to businessman Gary Pelzer. The couple have a daughter, Alexes Marie.

∽

Martha Byrne

Martha Byrne portrays the popular Lily Grimaldi on *As the World Turns.* She joined the series in 1985, left in 1989, and returned in 1993. She has received four Emmy Award nominations and won the award for Outstanding Ingenue in 1987.

Byrne was seen on Broadway at age ten, as July, one of the orphans in *Annie.* She starred in two feature films based on children's novels, *The Eyes of the Amaryllis* and *Anna to the Infinite Power.* On prime-time TV her credits include *The Hamptons, Kate and Allie, In the Heat of the Night, Jake and the Fatman, Silk Stalkings*, and *Murder, She Wrote.*

Byrne is a singer who has performed in clubs all over the country and has recently released an eponymously titled album. She is a featured soloist on RCA's *A Soap Opera Christmas.* Byrne is also a hospital spokesperson and fund-raiser for the St. Jude Children's Research Hospital in Tennessee.

Byrne resides in New Jersey with her husband, police officer Michael McMahon.

Thom Christopher

Thom Christopher, who seems to have cornered the market in portraying charming villains, was last seen on daytime as the manipulative Dante Partou on *Loving.* Prior to that he was bad-guy Carlo Hesser (as well as his good-guy twin brother, Mortimer Bern) on *One Life to Live,* a role that earned him an Emmy Award as Outstanding Supporting Actor in 1992.

A graduate of New York's High School of Performing Arts, Christopher has a B.A. from Ithaca College. On Broadway, he received the Theater World Award and the Clarence Derwent Award for his role in *Noel Coward in Two Keys,* starring Hume Cronyn and Jessica Tandy. Other theater credits include *Caesar and Cleopatra, One Flew over the Cuckoo's Nest,* and, more recently, *The Sound of Music* (as Captain Von Trapp), *Triumph of Love,* and *Love Letters* for the Rogue Repertory Company. On prime-time television, Christopher is best known for his portrayal of Hawk on the series *Buck Rogers.*

Christopher lives in Manhattan with his wife, playwright and personal manager Judith Leverone. The couple are staunch supporters of various charities, including Broadway Cares/Equity Fights AIDS.

Linda Cook

The daughter of a chemical company executive, the Lubbock, Texas–born Linda Cook lived in several cities before the family settled in Atlanta, Georgia, when she was a teenager. While still in high school, she was accepted into the prestigious Atlanta Civic Ballet and toured with the company throughout the Southeast.

After joining Atlanta's Alliance Theater Company,

she went on to numerous roles in regional theater, eventually deciding to pursue her craft in New York City.

On Broadway, Cook has been seen in *Home Front* and *The Wager.* Other credits include *Tartuffe, Crimes of the Heart,* and *No Time Flat.* On daytime, she's been seen as Laurie Ann Karr (*Edge of Night*), Lucy Voight (*All My Children*), Cynthia Linders (*As the World Turns),* and *Loving's* Egypt Masters.

Cook lives in Manhattan with her husband, scenic designer Patrick Mann.

Patricia Elliott

Patricia Elliott's (Renée Buchanan, *One Life to Live*) Broadway debut in 1973 was certainly a fortuitous one. The production was Stephen Sondheim's *A Little Night Music* and the role was Countess Charlotte, which earned Elliott a Theater World Award, Drama Desk Award, and the Tony as Best Featured Actress in a Musical. She followed this success with another, the Pulitzer Prize–winning play *The Shadow Box,* which earned her a second Tony nomination.

Elliott has also headlined in numerous off-Broadway and repertory productions, including *Tartuffe, Misalliance,* and *Much Ado About Nothing.* Prime-time TV credits include *Spenser: For Hire* and *Hill Street Blues.*

The actress is proud of her work with Plays for Living, an organization which produces inspirational plays performed at schools, shelters, prisons, churches, and corporations. She sits on the organization's board of directors and has been active in fund-raising for the group.

Eileen Fulton

Before there was Erica Kane (*All My Children*) or Alexis Carrington Colby (*Dynasty*), there was *As the World Turns'* Lisa Miller (currently Grimaldi), soapdom's first "villainess," who's been played by Eileen Fulton since 1960.

In addition to *ATWT* (where Lisa has managed to mellow a bit over the years without losing any of her delicious bite), Fulton appeared in the short-lived, *ATWT* prime-time spin-off, *Our Private World,* and on Broadway in *Who's Afraid of Virginia Woolf.* Off-Broadway credits include *The Fantastiks* and *Nite Club Confidential.*

Fulton is an accomplished cabaret singer who performs frequently on both coasts. In May 1995, *As My World Still Turns* (Birch Lane Press) was published, a continuation of Fulton's memoirs from her first autobiography.

∽

Karen Lynn Gorney

Although many filmgoers first noticed Karen Lynn Gorney for her portrayal of Stephanie, John Travolta's dance partner, in *Saturday Night Fever,* she was already known to millions of soap fans as Tara Martin on *All My Children,* a role she played for nearly a decade (and revived for several weeks during the fall of 1995).

Onstage, Gorney starred in *Lunch Hour* and toured with the Kenley Players as Mina in *Dracula.* Off-Broadway she was seen in *No Small Miracle* at Primary Stages and *Shattered Mirror* at the Arielle. At the West Bank Downstairs Theatre, her credits include *Love Museum* and her own play, *Unconditional Communication.* Among her other films are *David and Lisa, Short Circuit,* and *The Hard Way.*

Gorney is finishing an album she began for EMI in London. It will include her own work as well as songs by her father, Jay Gorney, who wrote the music for "Brother, Can You Spare a Dime?" with lyricist E. Y. Harburg.

Rebecca Holden

Following her music education from North Texas State University where she majored in music, Rebecca Holden (formerly Elena Parsons, *General Hospital*) went to New York to further her voice studies. While there she was discovered by a talent agency, which led to magazine covers, national television commercials, and ultimately a television and film career in Los Angeles.

Contributors' Profiles

Perhaps best known for her co-starring role on *Knight Rider* with David Hasselhoff in the late 1980s, Holden has guest-starred on numerous prime-time series, including *Taxi, Night Court, Magnum, P.I.,* and *Remington Steele.*

As a singer, Holden has opened concerts for such popular country performers as Sawyer Brown, Lee Greenwood, Gary Morris, and Ronnie McDowell, and has appeared in music videos for the Statler Brothers and Ronnie Milsap. She's recorded several singles of her own, among them "License to Steal" and "The Truth Doesn't Always Rhyme."

More recently, Holden was seen as the co-host of *Dancing at the Hot Spots* for The Nashville Network, and, after appearing in a documentary about former Breck Girls, was active in a revamped ad campaign for the hair-care line in 1994.

James Kiberd

James Kiberd may not be a police-detective-turned-lawyer like his alter-ego, *All My Children*'s Trevor Dillon, but the two share many traits, particularly an intense love of life.

A native of Providence, Rhode Island, Kiberd painted portraits as a child and later studied art at the University of Pennsylvania School of Fine Arts. His work has won acclaim from such organizations as the New York State Council on the Arts, the National Endowment for the Arts, and the America the Beautiful Fund. He began acting in 1980 and has numerous regional theater credits, including *The Seagull* and *Barefoot in the Park*. In 1993 he received wide acclaim for the lead role in *Macbeth* at the Pennsylvania Shakespeare Festival.

Prior to *AMC*, Kiberd portrayed emotionally scarred Vietnam vet Mike Donovan on *Loving*. While on *Loving*, he met his wife, actress Susan Keith (formerly Shana Vochek Burnell). The couple live in a 120-year-old Victorian home in upstate New York. Kiberd is proud to be the national ambassador for UNICEF.

Wortham Krimmer

As Rev. Andrew Carpenter on *One Life to Live*, Krimmer has turned what could have been a stereotypical character into a multifaceted one. His acting career may not have happened, however, had he continued with his law studies at the University of California at Hastings. While there he began doing plays at various Bay Area theaters, including the Berkeley Stage Company. This led to a full scholarship to the American Conservatory Theatre. During his final year at ACT (from which he received an M.F.A.) Krimmer was cast in the role of Martin Zeiss on the prime-time series *Paper Chase*. Other TV credits include *Hill Street Blues, St. Elsewhere,* and a regular role on the syndicated *Family Medical Center*. Prior to *OLTL* Krimmer appeared on *Days of Our Lives* as Cal Winters.

Krimmer and his wife , Mary Ellen, have two children, Max and Tess.

Carol Lawrence

Carol Lawrence (who portrayed Angela Eckert on *General Hospital*) first gained international acclaim when she created the role of Maria in Leonard Bernstein's classic Broadway musical *West Side Story.* She recently returned to the Great White Way in the Tony Award-winning musical *Kiss of the Spider Woman,* playing the title role.

Other Broadway credits include *Nightlife, Saratoga, Subways Are for Sleeping,* and *I Do, I Do* (replacing Mary Martin). Additionally, Lawrence has starred in national touring productions of *Funny Girl, The Unsinkable Molly Brown, The Sound of Music, Sweet Charity, I Do, I Do,* and *Sugar Babies.* Her feature film credits include *A View from the Bridge* and *Amore.* On prime-time TV she has guest-starred on numerous series, including *Matt Houston* and *Murder, She Wrote.*

More recent projects include a week-long celebration of Leonard Bernstein's work held in spring 1994 at the Metropolitan Museum of Art, as well as hosting *In the Spotlight* on the TBN network.

Lawrence continues to perform in cabarets and concert halls, sometimes joined by her sons, Michael and Christopher Goulet.

෴

Kate Linder

If passengers on United Airlines thought their flight attendant bore an amazing resemblance to the character Esther Valentine of *The Young and the Restless,* they were right. For seven of her twelve years as the housekeeper-confidante of Kay Chancellor (Jeanne Cooper), Linder kept her day job flying the friendly skies.

While still a confirmed world traveler and tourist, Linder is pretty much "grounded" these days with her work on *Y&R,* which began with one line—"Dinner is served." Born in Pasadena, California, Linder was active in high school drama and has a degree in theater arts from San Francisco State University. Following her graduation, Linder remained in San Francisco, dividing her time between roles in stock and repertory theater in the Bay Area and her work with the airlines. In the late 1970s, Linder and her husband, Ronald Linder, a leading expert and authority on drug abuse, moved to L.A., when he accepted a position at UCLA. For her part, Linder quickly won roles on such series as *Bay City Blues* and *Archie Bunker's Place.*

Known for her devotion to charitable concerns, Linder is active with Love Is Feeding Everyone (LIFE) and is a celebrity spokesperson/fund-raising chairperson for Escalon, a Pasadena-based school for children with learning disabilities.

∾

Contributors' Profiles

Judith McConnell

A native of Pittsburgh, Pennsylvania, Judith McConnell (who portrayed Sophia Capwell on *Santa Barbara* during its eight-year run) graduated from Carnegie Mellon University.

McConnell appeared in several productions at the Pittsburgh Playhouse, while on daytime she was seen as Valerie Conway on *As the World Turns* and Augusta McLeod on *General Hospital.*

The actress resides on the West Coast with her young daughter, Gwendolyn.

Vanessa Marcil

Vanessa Marcil (Brenda Barrett, *General Hospital*) was born in San Diego, California, and raised in Palm Desert. Her family also lived in Anchorage, Alaska, when her father's business took him there.

After graduating from high school, Marcil moved to L.A., where she began modeling. She's been seen on the stage in a repertory theater production of *Cat on a Hot Tin Roof* and *Southern Rapture.* Her film credits include *Nana to the Beach.*

Marcil made her television debut when she joined *GH* in 1992.

❧

Joseph Mascolo

Born and raised in West Hartford, Connecticut, Joseph Mascolo (Stefano Di Mera, *Days of Our Lives*) was in the clarinet section of the Metropolitan Opera Orchestra when he made the transition to acting. Following an off-Broadway production of *The Threepenny Opera,* Mascolo was seen in the landmark off-Broadway production of *A View from the Bridge* and joined an ensemble that included Jon Voight as co-star and Dustin Hoffman as assistant director. He made his Broadway debut in *Dinner at Eight.* Subsequent Broadway credits include *That Championship Season* and, more recently, *Breaking Legs.*

On prime-time TV, Mascolo has appeared in *The Gangster Chronicles, Hill Street Blues,* and *Lou Grant.* Feature film credits include *Diary of a Mad Housewife, Sharkey's Machine, Heat,* and *Yes, Giorgio,* which afforded Mascolo the opportunity to sing a duet with Luciano Pavarotti.

An avid tennis player and patron of the arts, Mascolo can often be found relaxing in the rose garden of his hillside home in southern California.

❦

Contributors' Profiles

Tommy Michaels

Already a thespian by the time he was a preteen, Tommy Michaels (Timmy Hunter, *All My Children*) was seen on Broadway as Garouche in *Les Miserables* and as Winfield Joad in the revival of *The Grapes of Wrath.*

Michaels's regional credits include *Inheritance, The Music Man,* and *Peter Pan,* while on prime-time television he was seen in the movies *The Littlest Victims* and *Quiz Show.*

When he's not acting, the fifteen-year-old enjoys gymnastics, baseball, soccer, and basketball.

Shelley Taylor Morgan

The former host of *Pure Soap* (which was canceled in December 1994 after a year-and-a-half run on E! Entertainment Television; she remains with the network as a special correspondent) is a former soap star herself, having appeared as Lorena Sharpe on *General Hospital* and Angelica Deveraux on *Days of Our Lives.*

Morgan's other credits include *Archie Bunker's Place, Webster* and *Hunter,* in which she played the recurring character Kitty O'Hearn. The actress, who was born in West Virginia, is active with Friends of Animals, an organization that finds homes for lost pets.

Lisa Peluso

Lisa Peluso (formerly Ava Masters, *Loving*) began modeling in her native Philadelphia when she was four months old. By age five she was acting in TV commercials and four years later appeared on Broadway with Angela Lansbury in *Gypsy.* At age twelve she played John Travolta's sister in *Saturday Night Fever.*

On daytime, Peluso played Wendy Wilkins on *Search for Tomorrow* for nearly a decade. Other soap credits include *Love of Life, Somerset, As the World Turns,* and *One Life to Live* as Billie Giordano, a role she played just prior to joining *Loving* in September 1988.

Peluso and her husband, photographer Brad Guice, live in New York City.

Thaao Penghlis

Born in Australia of Greek heritage, Thaao Penghlis (formerly Tony Di Mera, *Days of Our Lives)* was working with the Australian diplomatic service when he went to New York and joined the Australian mission to the United Nations. It was during this time that he met director and acting coach Milton Katselas, also of Greek descent.

Within a year, Penghlis decided to pursue an acting career, serving both as student and assistant to Katselas. While studying acting at night, Penghlis earned his living during the day as an apprentice art dealer specializing in Chinese and eighteenth-century English art.

Penghlis made his stage debut at the Beverly Hills

Playhouse in California in the starring role in *Jockeys,* in which he subsequently starred off-Broadway. Other stage credits include *The Collection, The Lion in Winter,* and *No Exit,* while filmgoers have seen him in *Altered States, The Bell Jar,* and *Slow Dancing in the Big City.* On television, Penghlis has had roles in numerous TV and cable movies, including *Under Siege, Sadat, Memories of Midnight,* and *Emma, Queen of the South Seas.* He was featured in a 1980s version of *Mission Impossible;* daytime viewers first noticed him as Victor Cassadine on *General Hospital.*

Penghlis visits his extended family in Australia two to three times a year. He also owns a home in Athens, just a short walk from the Acropolis.

Sydney Penny

Sydney Penny first received critical acclaim for her acting when she portrayed the young Meggie (played as an adult by Rachel Ward) in the miniseries *The Thorn Birds.* Her performing debut, however, occurred several years earlier when the three-and-a-half-year-old Penny jumped up on stage (where she sang her own composition, "My Little Pony"), following a performance by her parents—country and western entertainers Hank and Shari Penny.

The actress, now in her twenties, has smoothly made the transition to adult roles with appearances on TV series and in such films as *Pale Rider, Running Away,* and *Bernadette.* Prior to her current, Emmy-nominated role as Julia Santos on *All My Children,* Penny portrayed B. J.

Walker on *Santa Barbara,* a stint which also earned her an Emmy nomination for Outstanding Younger Actress.

She lives in New York with her husband, Bob Powers.

Tonya Pinkins

Shortly before joining *All My Children* in May 1991 as attorney Livia Frye Cudahy (a role she played until 1995), Pinkins appeared onstage in Los Angeles in *Jelly's Last Jam.* Pinkins later re-created her role, Sweet Anita, in the Broadway version (which starred Gregory Hines), earning a Tony Award for Best Supporting Actress in a Musical.

A native of Chicago, Pinkins's regional theater credits include *Joe Turner's Come and Gone, A . . . My Name Is Alice,* and *Ain't Misbehavin'.* Her prime-time TV credits include *The Cosby Show, Law and Order,* and *Crime Story.* On daytime, she portrayed Heather Dalton on *As the World Turns* from 1984 to 1986.

Pinkins has two young sons, Maxx and Myles. She lives in Manhattan.

Mark Pinter

Mark Pinter (Grant Harrison, *Another World*) received a bachelor's degree in theater arts at Iowa State University, where he helped found the Old Creamery

Theater Company in Garrison, Iowa.

Pinter has guest-starred on such prime-time series as *Hunter* and *The Love Boat,* while his daytime credits include *Love of Life, Guiding Light, Loving,* and *As the World Turns* (as Brian McColl), where he met his wife, Colleen Zenk Pinter (Barbara Montgomery). The couple have appeared on stage together in a production of A. R. Gurney's *Love Letters.*

Margaret Reed

A native of Salinas, California, Margaret Reed (formerly Shannon O'Hara McKechnie, *As the World Turns*) received her B.A. in theater from the University of California at Santa Cruz. She later attended Cornell University on scholarship to complete her M.F.A. in acting.

Reed's regional theater credits include *All My Sons, Twelfth Night,* and *The Taming of the Shrew.* During her run as Helena in *A Midsummer Night's Dream* at Philadelphia's Walnut Theater, she auditioned for and won the newly created role of Shannon on *ATWT.*

In 1990 Reed left the series to return to the West Coast where she quickly booked roles on *Seinfeld, The Young Riders, Blossom, Empty Nest, Knots Landing,* and *Star Trek: The Next Generation.* She appeared opposite Peter Reckell (Bo Brady, *Days of Our Lives*) in *Misconduct Allowed,* and won the Drama-Logue Award for her performance in *Other People's Money.* In 1994 she returned to New York, Shannon, and *ATWT.*

Reed resides in New Jersey with her husband, actor-stockbroker Kenny Myles, and their young son, Zachary.

James Reynolds

After his tour of duty as a Marine in Vietnam, James Reynolds (Abe Carver, *Days of Our Lives*) enrolled in Topeka's (Kansas) Washburn University, majoring in prelaw and journalism. Told that the best place to meet women was the theater department, Reynolds began auditioning and discovered a passion for acting. He appeared in campus and local productions, eventually leaving school and heading to San Francisco, where he worked as an actor.

A family matter brought him back to his native Kansas, where he landed a post with the *Topeka Daily Capitol,* for which he covered the entertainment beat. A few years later Reynolds resumed acting with a repertory company in Colorado Springs, Colorado.

Reynolds eventually moved to L.A. and quickly amassed a list of guest-star credits on such series as *Room 227, Hart to Hart,* and *Diff'rent Strokes.* Continuing his interest in theater, Reynold's organized and ran the L.A. Repertory Theater for seven years.

Reynolds, who also appeared on *Generations* as Henry Marshall (earning himself an Emmy nomination as Outstanding Lead Actor) in between his two stints on *Days,* regularly tours colleges with his one-man show, *I, Too, Am America.*

Reynolds and his wife, Lisa Layng, have a teenaged son, Jed.

Alexia Robinson

Alexia Robinson, formerly Meg Lawson on *General Hospital,* was born and raised in Fort Lauderdale, Florida. In 1985 she traveled to Los Angeles, where she quickly landed guest-star appearances on such series as *Fame, Hill Street Blues,* and *What's Happening Now.* She was also seen in the motion picture *Total Recall* with Arnold Schwarzenegger.

Robinson, who is active in several charities that benefit the homeless, holds a degree in business administration from Florida State University.

Chris Robinson

Chris Robinson (formerly Jack Hamilton, *The Bold and the Beautiful*) is a true Renaissance man. In addition to his acting career, Robinson owns several businesses in Arizona: an orchid and organic vegetable garden, the Big Lake Trading Post (which also boasts an American Indian Museum and cultural center), and an art gallery. (He owns another gallery in Florida.)

Prior to *B&B,* Robinson played Jason Frame on *Another World* and spent several years on *General Hospital* as Rick Webber. He's appeared in a variety of prime-time series and feature films, and is slated to portray the actor Montgomery Clift in an upcoming film biography.

Robinson lives in Los Angeles with his life partner, Lesleigh, and their three sons. The actor has seven other children from previous relationships.

Elvera Roussel

Elvera Roussel (who spent five years as Hope Bauer Spaulding on *Guiding Light*) attended Hofstra University, where she appeared in such productions as *Hamlet, Sweet Charity,* and *The Madness of Lady Bright.*

On prime-time TV she was seen in *Police Story, The Cradle Will Fall* (as her *GL* character, Hope), *A Question of Sex,* and *Working Trash.* Regional theater credits include *The Glass Menagerie, Lovers,* and *The Lion in Winter.*

Through New York University Roussel has written, produced, and directed several independent films, including *Two Views* and *When Aunt Lucy Came for Christmas.*

Roussel resides on New York's Long Island.

Monika Schnarre

When Monika Schnarre was cast as model Ivana on *The Bold and the Beautiful* (a role she played from June 1994 to March 1995), she didn't have to do any research: Schnarre has been a professional model for several years, gracing over a hundred magazine covers internationally. (She was also the youngest model to appear in *Sports Illustrated*'s celebrated swimsuit issue.)

Born in Scarborough, a suburb of Toronto, Schnarre began modeling professionally as a teenager. In 1986 she represented Canada in the Supermodel of the World Contest, winning the title over dozens of contestants.

Prior to *B&B,* Schnarre appeared in the feature film

Waxwork II: Lost in Time and on *Designing Women.* She has also penned a book for teenagers called *Between You and Me* (Bantam-Seal).

Melody Thomas Scott

Melody Thomas Scott (Nikki Abbott, *The Young and the Restless)* began her career at age three, as a member of the Meglin Kiddies, which performed USO shows around southern California.

By the time she was eight, Scott was appearing in such feature films as *Marnie,* portraying Tippi Hedren's title character as a child. As a junior high school student, she was featured in the gothic, Civil war–era film *The Beguiled,* starring Clint Eastwood. (One of her fondest memories of the film is receiving a daily kiss from Eastwood.) Other film credits include *Dirty Harry* (again with Eastwood), *Posse,* and *The Shootist*—John Wayne's last film. On prime-time television, Scott has appeared in several series, including a recurring role on *The Waltons.* She's been with *Y&R* for over fifteen years.

Scott is married to *Y&R* executive producer Edward Scott, and the family includes her daughter Alexandra, eleven; his daughter Jennifer, twenty-one; and their daughter Elizabeth, five.

❧

Lauren-Marie Taylor

An original-cast member of *Loving* (which debuted in 1983 and is now known as *The City*), Lauren-Marie Taylor (who played Stacey Forbes until the character was murdered in July 1995, kicking off a major storyline) grew up in the South Bronx and graduated from the Loyola School in Manhattan, later attending Wagner College and NYU.

Prior to *Loving,* Taylor appeared in TV commercials and played John Belushi's daughter in the film *Neighbors.* On stage she's appeared in *Album* at New York's Cherry Lane Theater and at the Apollo Theater in Chicago.

Off screen Taylor is an accomplished long-distance runner who has consistently finished among the top women runners in the annual ABC, Inc., Corporate and Media Challenge Series races, held in New York City.

Taylor is married to songwriter John Didrichson. They live in New York's Hudson Valley with their three children, Katherine, Wesley, and Olivia.

Russell Todd

A native of New York, Russell Todd (Jerry Birn, *The Bold and the Beautiful*) spent three years on *Another World* in the contract role of Jamie Frame. Other daytime credits include *The Young and the Restless, All My Children,* and *The Doctors.* On prime-time TV he was a series regular on *High Mountain Rangers* and has guest-starred on such programs as *Jake and the Fatman* and *Riptide*. Film credits include *Where the Boys Are '84, Sweet Murder,* and *Night Hawks.*

Todd attended Syracuse University. He and his wife, Kim, a schoolteacher, live on the West Coast.

Kristina Wagner

Kristina Wagner was Kristina Malandro when she joined *General Hospital* in 1985 as Aztec Princess Felicia Jones. But in true soap opera–style, she fell in love and married her co-star, Jack Wagner (Frisco Jones). The couple have two sons, Peter John and Harrison Hale.

A native of Indianapolis, Wagner attended Indiana Central University and Indiana University as a theater arts major. After appearing in local commercials, Wagner's big break came when she answered an audition call for the part of Felicia.

During a self-imposed hiatus from *GH* in the late 1980s, Wagner visited Africa, where she became committed to increasing public awareness of the crisis facing African wildlife.

∼

Jacklyn Zeman

Born in Englewood, New Jersey, Jacklyn Zeman (Bobbie Jones, *General Hospital*) was attending New York University as a dance major when she suddenly decided that she wanted to act on a daytime drama. Within three months of enrolling in a drama school, Zeman made her debut on *One Life to Live.* After her character on that soap came to an untimely end, Zeman joined *GH* in 1977.

Zeman has appeared in several motion pictures, including *Young Doctors in Love* and *National Lampoon's Class Reunion.* She regularly makes guest appearances on talk and game shows, and has been a co-host of *The Home Show.* In 1986 she penned *Beauty on the Go* for Simon & Schuster, later turning the book into a home video.

Zeman and her husband, Glenn Gorden, have two daughters, Cassidy and Lacey.

∾

Grateful acknowledgment is made to the following individuals
and organizations for permission to reprint photographs:

∾

Robert Milazzo Photography. Julia Barr, Thom Christopher, Lisa
Peluso, Sydney Penny, Mark Pinter

Herb Polsky. Brenda Brock

Lesley Bohm. Kimberlin Brown

Robin Platzer/Twin Images. Wortham Krimmer, Tommy Michaels,
Tonya Pinkins, Margaret Reed

Leslie Burke/Gamma Liaison. Kate Linder

Rob Lewine. Judith McConnell

Courtesy Patricia Marcil. Vanessa Marcil

John Paschal/Celebrity Photo. Joseph Mascolo

Courtesy E! Entertainment Television. Shelley Taylor Morgan

Courtesy The Garrett Co. Thaao Penghlis, James Reynolds

Craig Skinner/Celebrity Photo. Alexia Robinson

Geraldine Overton/CBS-TV. Melody Thomas Scott

Lisa O'Connor/Celebrity Photo. Kristina Wagner

Index

African chicken with peanuts,
20–21
Aimee's (my grandmother) apple
pie, 88–89
Alexia's lemon chicken tenders,
24–25
Alexia's stuffed mushrooms, 2–3
Allison's vegetable pasta salad,
50–51
All My Children, 20, 34, 50, 74, 95,
101, 102, 103, 104, 110,
112, 113
Another World, 60, 113, 120
appetizers:
   Alexia's stuffed mushrooms, 2–3
   Vanessa's salsa, 6
apple:
   cranberry delight, 82–83
   pie, Aimee's (my grandmother),
      88–89
   sausage dressing, James
      Reynolds's spicy, 64–65
As the World Turns, 40, 44, 78, 99,
101, 102, 114

Aunt Carolyn's pumpkin pie, 86–87
Auntie's low-fat fish casserole,
34–35
Aunt Irma's kugel (noodle
pudding), 92–93

Bacon, in Melody Thomas Scott's
layered Southern salad, 4–5
Baja Laguna trout, Brother Buck's,
32–33
banana split pie, 84–85
Barr, Julia, 50–51, 95
beans:
   black or red, and tortilla
      casserole, 40–41
   in Monika's minestrone, 10–11
   pasta e fagioli, 46–47
   pinto, Portuguese style, 42–43
Bell, Lauralee, 72–73, 96
black bean and tortilla casserole,
40–41
Bold and the Beautiful, The, 10, 42,
52, 80, 82, 90, 98, 116, 118,
120

breads:
    chocolate chip, 80–81
    cornbread, 76
    Kate Linder's pumpkin, 58–59
    Katie's corn muffins, 60–61
broccoli, in Allison's vegetable
        pasta salad, 50–51
Brock, Brenda, 32–33, 97
Brother Buck's Baja Laguna trout,
        32–33
Brown, Kimberlin, 42–43, 52–53,
        90–91, 98
Byrne, Martha, 78–79, 99

Café Creevey, jelled, 94
cake, chocolate icebox, 78–79
cannellini and pasta, 46–47
casserole:
    Auntie's low-fat fish, 34–35
    Lauralee Bell's egg surprise,
        72–73
    tortilla and black or red bean,
        40–41
cheese melt, tomato-tuna, 74–75
chicken:
    African, with peanuts, 20–21
    Alexia's lemon, tenders, 24–25
    cordon bleu, 26–27
    in escarole soup, 7–9
    King Ranch, 16–17
    Martiniquaise, Melody Thomas
        Scott's, 22–23
    with orange, 18–19
chocolate:
    chip bread, 80–81
    icebox cake, 78–79
Christopher, Thom, 94, 99–100
clams, cherrystone, in Thaao
        Penghlis's pasta and
        seafood, 30–31

comfort foods:
    cornbread, 76
    Grandma Sadie Stone Cook's
        West Texas sweetheart
        salad, 70–71
    James Reynolds's spicy apple
        sausage dressing, 64–65
    Kate Linder's pumpkin bread,
        58–59
    Kate Linder's Thanksgiving
        sweet potato eggnog
        pudding, 66–67
    Katie's corn muffins, 60–61
    Lauralee Bell's egg surprise,
        72–73
    Mark Pinter's hiccup-hot red
        pepper jelly, 62–63
    sweet potato oranges, 68–69
    tomato-tuna cheese melt, 74–75
Cook, Linda, 70–71, 100–101
cordon bleu, chicken, 26–27
cornbread, 76
corn muffins, Katie's, 60–61
crabmeat, in Alexia's stuffed
        mushrooms, 2–3
cranberry apple delight, 82–83
cream and peaches pie, Kimberlin
        Brown's, 90–91

Days of Our Lives, 18, 30, 64, 109,
        110, 111, 115
desserts:
    Aimee's (my grandmother)
        apple pie, 88–89
    Aunt Carolyn's pumpkin pie,
        88–89
    Aunt Irma's kugel (noodle
        pudding), 92–93
    banana split pie, 84–85
    chocolate chip bread, 80–81

chocolate icebox cake, 78–79
cranberry apple delight, 82–83
jelled café Creevey, 94
Kate Linder's Thanksgiving
    sweet potato eggnog
    pudding, 66–67
Kimberlin Brown's peaches and
    cream pie, 90–91
sweet potato oranges, 68–69
dressing, James Reynolds's spicy
    apple sausage, 64–65

Eggnog sweet potato pudding,
    Kate Linder's Thanksgiving,
    66–67
egg surprise, Lauralee Bell's, 72–73
Elliott, Patricia, 12–13, 54–55,
    68–69, 101–102
escarole soup, 7–9

Fagioli e pasta, 46–47
fettuccine, in Allison's vegetable
    pasta salad, 50–51
fish:
    Brother Buck's Baja Laguna
        trout, 32–33
    casserole, Auntie's low-fat, 34–35
    pasta con tonno alla Trevor,
        48–49
    sole in tomato sauce, 36–37
    Thaao Penghlis's pasta and
        seafood, 30–31
    tomato-tuna cheese melt, 74–75
flounder, in Auntie's low-fat fish
    casserole, 34–35
Fulton, Eileen, 40–41, 102

General Hospital, 2, 6, 16, 24, 28,
    36, 38, 46, 84, 86, 103, 106,
    108, 110, 116, 120, 121

Gorney, Karen Lynn, 34–35, 103
Grandma Sadie Stone Cook's West
    Texas sweetheart salad,
    70–71
gratin, spinach and rice, 44–45
Guiding Light, 92, 117

Ham, in chicken cordon bleu,
    26–27
hiccup-hot red pepper jelly, Mark
    Pinter's, 62–63
hijiki heaven, 54–55
Holden, Rebecca, 16–17, 84–85,
    103–104

Icebox cake, chocolate, 78–79

Jalapeño peppers:
    in Mark Pinter's hiccup-hot red
        pepper jelly, 60–61
    in Vanessa's salsa, 6
James Reynolds's spicy apple
    sausage dressing, 64–65
jelled café Creevey, 94
jelly, Mark Pinter's hiccup-hot red
    pepper, 62–63

Kate Linder's pumpkin bread,
    58–59
Kate Linder's Thanksgiving sweet
    potato eggnog pudding,
    66–67
Katie's corn muffins, 60–61
Kiberd, James, 48–49, 104–105
kidney beans and pasta, 46–47
Kimberlin Brown's famous pesto,
    52–53
Kimberlin Brown's peaches and
    cream pie, 90–91
King Ranch chicken, 16–17

Krimmer, Wortham, 76, 105
kugel (noodle pudding), Aunt
    Irma's, 92–93

Lauralee Bell's egg surprise, 72–73
Lawrence, Carol, 28–29, 46–47, 106
layered Southern salad, Melody
    Thomas Scott's, 4–5
lemon chicken tenders, Alexia's,
    24–25
Linder, Kate, 58–59, 66–67, 107
linguine:
    in pasta con tonno alla Trevor,
        48–49
    in Thaao Penghlis's pasta and
        seafood, 30–31
Loving, 7, 60, 70, 94, 99, 111, 119
low-fat dish casserole, Auntie's,
    34–35

McConnell, Judith, 88–89, 108
Marcil, Vanessa, 6, 108
Mark Pinter's hiccup-hot red
    pepper jelly, 62–63
Mascolo, Joseph, 18–19, 109
Melody Thomas Scott's chicken
    Martiniquaise, 22–23
Melody Thomas Scott's layered
    Southern salad, 4–5
Michaels, Tommy, 74–75, 110
minestrone, Monika's, 10–11
Morgan, Shelley Taylor, 38–39, 110
muffins, Katie's corn, 60–61
mushrooms, Alexia's stuffed, 2–3

Noodle pudding, Aunt Irma's
    kugel, 92–93

One Life to Live, 12, 32, 54, 68,
    76, 97, 101, 105

orange(s):
    chicken with, 18–19
    sweet potato, 68–69

Pasta:
    e fagioli, 46–47
    and seafood, Thaao Penghlis's,
        30–31
    con tonno alla Trevor, 48–49
    vegetable salad, Allison's, 50–51
peaches and cream pie, Kimberlin
    Brown's, 90–91
peanuts, African chicken with,
    20–21
Peluso, Lisa, 7–9, 111
Penghlis, Thaao, 30–31, 111
Penny, Sydney, 26–27, 112–113
pepper, red, jelly, Mark Pinter's
    hiccup-hot, 62–63
pesto, Kimberlin Brown's famous,
    52–53
pies:
    Aimee's (my grandmother)
        apple, 88–89
    Aunt Carolyn's pumpkin, 86–87
    banana split, 84–85
    Kimberlin Brown's peaches and
        cream, 90–91
pineapple salsa verde, 33
pink delight, 12–13
Pinkins, Tonya, 20–21, 113
Pinter, Mark, 62–63, 113–114
pinto beans Portuguese style,
    42–43
Portuguese style pinto beans,
    42–43
potato, sweet:
    eggnog pudding, Kate Linder's
        Thanksgiving, 66–67
    oranges, 68–69

puddings:
  Aunt Irma's kugel (noodle),
    92–93
  Kate Linder's Thanksgiving
    sweet potato eggnog, 66–67
pumpkin:
  bread, Kate Linder's, 58–59
  pie, Aunt Carolyn's, 86–87

Red bean and tortilla casserole,
    40–41
red pepper jelly, Mark Pinter's
    hiccup-hot, 62–63
Reed, Margaret, 44–45, 114–115
Reynolds, James, 64–65, 115–116
rice and spanish gratin, 44–45
Robinson, Alexia, 2–3, 24–25,
    116
Robinson, Chris, 80–81, 116–117
Roussel, Elvera, 92–93, 117

Salads:
  Allison's vegetable pasta,
    50–51
  Grandma Sadie Stone Cook's
    West Texas sweetheart,
    70–71
  Melody Thomas Scott's layered
    Southern, 4–5
salsa, Vanessa's, 6
salsa verde, pineapple, 33
Santa Barbara, 88, 108
sauce:
  Kimberlin Brown's famous
    pesto, 52–53
  pineapple salsa verde, 33
  tomato, sole in, 36–37
  Vanessa's salsa, 6
sausage spicy apple dressing,
    James Reynolds's, 64–65

scallops:
  in Alexia's stuffed mushrooms,
    2–3
  in Thaao Penghlis's pasta and
    seafood, 30–31
scampi, shrimp, 28–29
Schnarre, Monika, 10–11, 118
Scott, Melody Thomas, 4, 22–23,
    118–119
seafood:
  and pasta, Thaao Penghlis's,
    30–31
  shrimp scampi, 28–29
  see also fish
Shelley Taylor Morgan's stroganoff
    for lovers, 38–39
shrimp:
  in Alexia's stuffed mushrooms,
    2–3
  in pink delight, 12–13
  scampi, 28–29
  in Thaao Penghlis's pasta and
    seafood, 30–31
sole:
  in Auntie's low-fat fish casserole,
    34–35
  in tomato sauce, 36–37
soups:
  escarole, 7–9
  Monika's minestrone, 10–11
  pink delight, 12–13
Southern salad, Melody Thomas
    Scott's layered, 4–5
spicy apple sausage dressing,
    James Reynolds's, 64–65
spinach and rice gratin, 44–45
stroganoff for lovers, Shelley
    Taylor Morgan's, 38–39
stuffed mushrooms, Alexia's,
    2–3

127   Index

sweetheart salad, Grandma Sadie
    Stone Cook's West Texas,
    70–71
sweet potato:
  eggnog pudding, Kate Linder's
    Thanksgiving, 66–67
  oranges, 68–69

Taylor, Lauren-Marie, 60–61,
    119–120
Thaao Penghlis's pasta and
    seafood, 30–31
Thanksgiving sweet potato eggnog
    pudding, Kate Linder's,
    66–67
Todd, Russell, 82–83, 120
tomato:
  sauce, sole in, 36–37
  -tuna cheese melt, 74–75
tortilla and black or red bean
    casserole, 40–41
trout, Brother Buck's Baja Laguna,
    32–33
tuna:
  pasta con tonno alla Trevor,
    48–49
  -tomato cheese melt, 74–75

Vanessa's salsa, 6
vegetarian main dishes:
  Allison's vegetable pasta salad,
    50–51
  hijiki heaven, 54–55
  pasta e fagioli, 46–47
  pasta salad, Allison's, 50–51
  spinach and rice gratin, 44–45
  tortilla and black or red bean
    casserole, 40–41

Wagner, Kristina, 86–87,
    120–121
water chestnuts, in Melody
    Thomas Scott's layered
    Southern salad, 4–5
West Texas sweetheart salad,
    Grandma Sadie Stone
    Cook's, 70–71

Young and the Restless, The, 4, 22,
    58, 66, 72, 96, 107, 118,
    120

Zeman, Jacklyn, 36–37, 122